Something beautiful occurs when we set ourselves aside and bask in the shining glory of Christ. In *From Glory to Glory*, Bob Santos magnificently demonstrates the implications of soaking in the presence of the King of Glory. We begin to discover our true worth as we identify ourselves as children of God. All the while, Jesus continually restores our fragmented glory, satisfies our glory deficiencies, and shows us how loved we truly are.

—Samantha Carey
Spoken Word Poet
Indiana, PA

Bob Santos, in his book *From Gory to Glory*, gives us a fresh new perspective in the spiritual struggle to discover who we are designed to be in the midst of a world full of self-glorification. Bob's insights into the Scriptures and the nature of God are deep and meaningful. Whether you are a new or seasoned believer, each bite-sized chapter is chock-full of truth designed to both challenge and encourage you on your spiritual journey to the glory of God.

—Dr. Carl Forster
Reach Out Church
Hyde Park, NY

Bookstores, both religious and non-religious, are full of "self-help" books, most of which overlook the fundamental issue which had caused one to seek help in the first place. Bob Santos, in his book, guides the reader to realize the fundamental problem—that which he calls a "glory deficiency"—and then helps the reader to address the deficiency in a healthy and lasting manner. I highly recommend this book to all who have the courage to look deeply within and then look to the One who alone can satisfy.

—Tom Brazell
Elim Fellowship
Wellsville, NY

After serving the Lord in Christian leadership for over twenty years, along came Bob Santos' book to open my eyes afresh to the identity I have in Christ. With Bob's thought-provoking stories and questions, *From Glory to Glory* propels my faith to new heights, and fills my heart with gratitude for the reality of what Jesus Christ has done for us.

—Sandy Hempfling
Youth With A Mission
Arvada, CO

From Glory to Glory is more than a road map to transformation. It highlights truths that will direct the reader to freedom and significance. This insightful guide will lead you to a restoration of validation that comes from personal revelation. I challenge you to read this book and enjoy the journey of transformation that comes from true glory.

—Chaplain Debi Adams, BCC
Torrance State Hospital
Torrance, PA

Experiencing the glory of God on earth can be easily realized and daily witnessed by followers of Jesus Christ. I believe that knowing and understanding those experiences is the center pin to our great and growing relationship with God. In his book *From Glory to Glory*, Bob Santos guides us through that divine relationship, and therefore into a deeper understanding of His glory in us.

—Matt Geppert
SEAPC
Oakmont, PA

From Glory to Glory is a spot-on word for this hour to the Body of Christ. In it, Bob Santos unpacks the deep journey into the restoration of identity which every heart craves but often does not see take place. We must not stop at moments of revival or temporary glory resting on us. We must go forward into possessing restoration of who we are in Him, and the enduring glory we are born to live in and release. *From Glory to Glory* leads you to this place!

—John Paul Sprecher
SEAPC
Oakmont, PA

In his book *From Glory to Glory*, Bob Santos takes a thoughtful and provoking look into human identity and its pathway to majesty. Bob's faithful dedication does not provide mere motivation, but a revelation that will release you to live with boldness of faith.

—Jason Betler
The Nations Hope
Singapore

From Glory to Glory is a great read if you want to go deeper in your walk. This book has everything you need to know about walking in His glory. If you have ever wondered what glory does or what being in His glory means, you are reading the right book. Bob does an excellent job of diving into the Scriptures and giving you a complete overview of His glory. This is a must read!

—Ricky Ingram
Summit Church
Indiana, PA

Bob Santos is not just a deep thinker; he is a reflective thinker, meaning that he is not shy about allowing the light of truth to penetrate the fog of our understanding about who we are. *From Glory to Glory* reflects on what most of us deal with throughout life: a search for identity and significance. The book takes this search through many different social and cultural expressions to the ultimate source for everything that everyone seeks and needs in life.

—Gary Ham
The Eleventh Hour Christian Initiatives
Rochester, NY

Every person on the planet searches for real significance. In *From Glory to Glory*, Bob Santos helps us understand why our need for it is so great, reveals why what the world has to offer can never fill the void, and powerfully leads us to the only One who can quench our thirst. This forty-day devotional is a must read for all generations!

—Josh Rendulic
Hope Fellowship
Chestertown, MD

Hungry for glory? In Bob's most recent pearl, he helps us to recognize that we are all hungry for glory. We search and claw, but our desire will only be truly satisfied and glory restored in relationship with Jesus. Like his previous work, *Champions in the Wilderness*, Bob again offers meaty Biblical content and relatable stories, formatted as a devotional that can be savored daily. If you've struggled to understand your true identity, take this journey with Bob from shame to glory and discover real freedom in Christ.

—Johanna Beatty
MA Pastoral Counseling, Victim Advocate
Indiana, PA

From Glory to Glory

"For the earth will be filled
With the knowledge of the glory of the Lord,
As the waters cover the sea."
Habakkuk 2:14

From Glory to Glory

Finding Real Significance in an Image-Driven World

BOB SANTOS

SEARCH FOR ME MINISTRIES, INC.
INDIANA, PA

From Glory to Glory:
Finding Real Significance in an Image-Driven World
By Bob Santos

Copyright © 2018, 2024 by Search for Me Ministries, Inc.
Revised First Edition

Cover Photo: Cynthia Leidlein
Cover Design: Gaffney Printables
Interior Design: Bob Santos
Editor: Crystal Min (crystalclearenglish.com)

Unless otherwise noted, all Scripture quotations are taken from the New American Standard Bible® (NASB), Copyright © 1960, 1962, 1963, 1968, 1971, 1972, 1973, 1975, 1977, 1995 by The Lockman Foundation. Used by permission. (www.Lockman.org) Quotations from the Old Testament are capitalized.

Scripture quotations marked (HCSB) are taken from the Holman Christian Standard Bible®, Copyright © 1999, 2000, 2002, 2003 by Holman Bible Publishers. Used by permission. Holman Christian Standard Bible®, Holman CSB®, and HCSB® are federally registered trademarks of Holman Bible Publishers.

Scripture quotations marked (NLT) are taken from the Holy Bible, New Living Translation, Copyright © 1996, 2004, 2007, 2013, 2015 by Tyndale House Foundation. Used by permission of Tyndale House Publishers, Inc., Carol Stream, Illinois 60188. All rights reserved.

Published by SfMe Media
Indiana, PA 15701
www.sfme.org

Printed in the United States of America

Library of Congress Control Number for previous edition: 2018904641

ISBN: 978-1-937956-16-5
ePub ISBN: 978-1-937956-17-2

To those seemingly obscure souls who have paid a steep price for the benefit of others. Of them, this world is not worthy.

CONTENTS

Introduction	13
Phase One: Discerning Image vs. Substance	15
1. Faltering Glory	17
2. More Than an Opinion	21
3. The King of Glory	25
4. The Glory of His Presence	29
5. The Ultimate Temptation	33
6. Naked and Ashamed	37
7. Fig Leaves	41
8. The Day of Ichabod	45
9. Nothing but Possum Glory	49
10. The Pale Blue Dot	53
Phase One Reflections	57
Phase Two: Seeing Why Identity Matters	59
11. Glory as a Drug	61
12. Stairways to Heaven?	65
13. Sin and Significance	69
14. Rejection Hurts	73
15. Cancerous Insecurity	77
16. Opened but Closed	81
17. My Kingdom Over Yours	85
18. The Social Righteousness Trap	89
19. Roots of Conflict	93
20. Free from the Glory Quest	97
Phase Two Reflections	101

Phase Three: Finding Real Significance — 103

21. In His Image — 105
22. In Our Image — 109
23. The Father Heart of God — 113
24. Becoming A Child of God — 117
25. The Covenant Family of God — 121
26. Chosen by God — 125
27. The Apple of His Eye — 129
28. Intimacy with God — 133
29. New Creatures in Christ — 137
30. Never Abandoned — 141

Phase Three Reflections — 145

Phase Four: Seeking True Glory — 147

31. Our Hope of Glory — 149
32. A Royal Priesthood — 153
33. The Bride of Christ — 157
34. Kingdom Ambassadors — 161
35. Joint Heirs with Christ — 165
36. Seated in Heavenly Places — 169
37. Glory out of Weakness — 173
38. The High Road of Humility — 177
39. Hidden Glory — 181
40. Hearts of Worship — 185

Phase Four Reflections — 189

Final Reflections — 191

Appendix — 193

INTRODUCTION

I have thoughtfully studied the Biblical perspective of identity for many years, and before I started writing this book, I thought I had a pretty good grasp on the topic. Now, as I place the finishing touches on my labor of love, I realize how limited my perspective has been.

Identity is a complex issue that we have seen addressed by psychologists, sociologists, and increasingly, it seems, church leaders. The rich, intellectually stimulating subject of identity has absorbed my focus for almost two decades. Only recently, however, did I realize that the essential connection between glory—a major theme woven through practically every page of the Bible—and identity was missing from both my understanding and much of the literature I have read. To be honest, at first, I struggled even to define the concept of glory.

The issues in this book are some of the most important we could ever choose to explore. Why? How we view ourselves, including the sources from which we draw our sense of significance, influences virtually every area of our lives. Make no mistake; glory is a huge issue for us even if we struggle to define its meaning.

While an inner quest for significance is common to all humans, the means by which we seek validation profoundly influences our well-being. We either look to God to define the meaning and value of our lives, or we "go rogue," seeking a sense of identity through self-effort and human approval. *Not until we learn to align our motivations with our Creator's wise design will we establish a truly healthy sense of personal significance.*

The personal nature of glory means that dealing with the issue also presents significant challenges. We do not always appreciate even well-intentioned attempts to address the self-fabricated narratives of our persons. But if we want to be whole and free, we must learn to look beyond our own limited perspectives.

Yes, this book will walk you through some uncomfortable and potentially painful issues, but we will not pitch a tent and set up camp there. Instead, we will explore and process the contrast between fading and lasting glory, come face-to-face with the dysfunction our human approach creates, and then move into the sweetness of God's goodness toward us.

His approach, you see, is not as negative as we are often led to believe. Yes, our Creator has wisely designed the Christian gospel (meaning "good news") to thoroughly deal with the ills of humanity, but that is not where the focus remains. From a Biblical perspective, death might precede life, but life is always the good Lord's ultimate goal.

In a similar vein, we dare never forget the dire reality of our past sins, and yet our human failures cannot be our focus. Otherwise, we elevate the bad over the good, the ignoble over the noble, and the shameful over the magnificent. How we must learn to see ourselves—and others—through God's wise and loving eyes! All that He desires for us is truly glorious, amazing in every way.

As we will soon see, humanity's problems began with a quest for independence from our Creator. I cannot, therefore, even begin to think about adequately addressing the concept of identity apart from the Bible. Thus, I have written this book as though the typical reader were Christian while doing my best to limit the use of common Christian jargon for the sake of a broader audience.

If you are in the process of exploring the Christian faith and are unsure of what that entails, I suggest turning to the Appendix. It provides a basic understanding of how to become part of God's royal family.

Finally, I have used a devotional format to break deep, complex issues into "bite-sized chunks" that should be prayerfully processed, not hurried through. Glory is a deep concept that requires both thoughtful contemplation and personal reflection, neither of which can be accomplished in an instant.

Writing this book has opened my eyes and facilitated deep-rooted healing in my life. I hope and pray that you benefit even more than I did as you embark on this journey of discovery and truth.

Bob Santos

January 2024 Revision: After over five years in print, I felt the need to make some changes. Most are stylistic. Bob

PHASE ONE
DISCERNING IMAGE VS. SUBSTANCE

> A voice is calling,
> "Clear the way for the Lord in the wilderness;
> Make smooth in the desert a highway for our God.
> Let every valley be lifted up,
> And every mountain and hill be made low;
> And let the rough ground become a plain,
> And the rugged terrain a broad valley;
> Then the glory of the Lord will be revealed,
> And all flesh will see it together;
> For the mouth of the Lord has spoken."
> A voice says, "Call out."
> Then he answered, "What shall I call out?"
> All flesh is grass, and all its loveliness is like the flower of the field.
> The grass withers, the flower fades,
> When the breath of the Lord blows upon it;
> Surely the people are grass.
> The grass withers, the flower fades,
> But the word of our God stands forever.
> Isaiah 40:3–8

In this first phase of our journey, we will explore the stark contrast between fading and lasting glory, along with an understanding of how our human perspectives became skewed. This thought-provoking endeavor will open our eyes to see the writings of the Bible in a fascinating new light.

DAY ONE
FALTERING GLORY

Their inner thought is that their houses are forever
And their dwelling places to all generations;
They have called their lands after their own names.
But man in his pomp will not endure;
He is like the beasts that perish.

Psalm 49:11–12

"It burst into flames!... It's fire. And it's crashing, it's crashing terrible!... Oh, the humanity."

—Herbert Morrison

The date was May 6, 1937, and radio broadcaster Herbert Morrison fought back tears—a stream of anguished words cascading from his gaping jaw. The proud Nazi airship Hindenburg had just ignited and crashed to the ground at Naval Air Station Lakehurst in Manchester Township, New Jersey. In a matter of seconds, the fiery crash extinguished thirty-six human lives. This tragedy also marked the culmination of the short but illustrious reign of hydrogen-laden airships as the preferred form of travel.

The LZ 129 Hindenburg had briefly represented the height of human glory as felt by Adolf Hitler and his Third Reich. Not only did precious works of art adorn silk wallpaper in the dining area, the silver airship even boasted a lightweight baby grand piano as it sped back and forth across the Atlantic during its 1936 travel season.

Feeling the elation of rising glory, Nazi leaders employed the Hindenburg to blare patriotic music—while dropping propaganda leaflets and swastika flags—during a four-day tour of Germany. At the 1936 Summer Olympic Games in Berlin, the magnificent airship starred in the opening ceremonies as a luxurious, aerodynamic wonder to display the supposed Nazi superiority to the world.

The correlation between the demise of the illustrious airship and that of Nazi Germany should not be missed. Eerie film footage of the word "Hindenburg" being consumed by flames accurately reflects the final fate of Adolf Hitler and his ill-fated Third Reich. On every level, Nazi glory was but a temporary image unable to stand the tests of time and adversity.

Despite his twisted character and systematic elimination of political opponents, much of the civilized world once viewed Hitler in a favorable light. Why? Just as we see in our modern times, skilled propaganda experts had crafted a careful and highly effective public relations campaign. On August 20, 1939, twelve days before Germany invaded Poland, the New York Times ran a favorable article calling Hitler a "country gentleman." The Times was not the only publication duped. According to an interview by Charlotte Hsu with Despina Stratigakos, author of *Hitler at Home*:

> "By the end of the 1930s, news stories around the world described him as a caring, gentle individual with great taste in home décor...It was dangerous because it made him likeable," Stratigakos said. "After reading these stories, people would feel like they knew the 'true' Hitler, the private man behind the Führer mask, and that maybe this person was not as bad as all of the news coming out of Europe seemed to suggest."[1]

Adolf Hitler and his publicists had carefully crafted a warm public persona by publishing sparkling images of the cold-hearted dictator with majestic dogs, adorable children, and a tastefully decorated mountain estate, tomato garden included. History tells us, however, that Hitler's public image was a bold-faced lie, betrayed by his sinister pogroms. In addition to the tens of millions of people killed through the global war launched by the Nazis and their Axis allies, Hitler's regime mercilessly executed about six million Jews. My Uncle Mick was one of the Allied soldiers who helped liberate the Dachau concentration camp, and the graphic images thrust upon him left an indelible mark on his psyche.

---

1. Charlotte Hsu, "How media 'fluff' helped Hitler rise to power," University at Buffalo News Center (August 28, 2015), accessed April 2, 2024, http://www.buffalo.edu/news/releases/2015/08/034.html.

That the civilized world widely recognizes the depravity of the Nazi regime makes a significant statement about our collective sense of morality. At the same time, I am compelled to join many others in questioning the root motivations of the Nazi's extreme behavior. Are we talking about the bizarre actions of only a twisted few, or are we dealing with natural inclinations that have long been part of our human DNA? Most of us tend to think of Hitler as an anomaly of civilization. But while his heinous actions were no doubt extreme, the root inclinations toward power, control, and self-elevation form a universal aspect of human nature that we dare not ignore.

Is it possible that sinister roots creep their way through the fabric of human civilization, only to produce the fullness of an evil harvest when the "right" circumstances converge? After all, Adolf Hitler could have never done so much damage on his own; he was supported by millions of people in the Nazi party who shared his ideology and many more who passively allowed him to act.

As much as the Nazi regime stands out for the scope of its atrocities, none of us are so foolish to believe that their motivations were unique. This planet's soil is stained with the blood of brutality, and to this day ruthless men and women wreak havoc across the globe, driven by a never-ending lust for power and glory.

Diversity might abound in our world, but so does similarity. Whether we speak of the oppressors or the oppressed, all who call themselves "human" share the same basic desires for happiness, meaning, and freedom. Sadly, all are also subject to traits, which if not handled wisely, will create all manner of dysfunction. In particular, I refer to our ever-present craving for *glory*. Or should I say significance? Or validation? Or honor? Or renown? Or prestige? Each is simply a nuanced expression of the same basic concept.

Deep within every human heart stirs a virtually unquenchable appetite for affirmation, approval, and adulation. Everyone wants to be somebody, no exceptions. Furthermore, it is not enough to simply be somebody; we want to be **somebody**—to be elevated in an admirable, superior light. And God help those ignoble souls who fail to meet the human standards required to garner applause, or at the very least, to avoid being ostracized. A miserable existence is their lot as they wistfully wish for a status beyond their grasp.

The humanity of it all! Why does glory mean so much to our social and emotional existence? Why are we so prone to desire superiority? Why do we struggle with feelings of insecurity? Why does the approval—or disapproval—of others mean so much to us? Why does it even matter if we feel significant?

I propose that we are all spiritual creatures, created in God's image and "wired" for glory. I refer not to a vain quest for the short-lived applause of human approval, but to the firm and lasting substance of significance that flows only from heaven's throne. Human glory is a sad substitute for the divine, and though we are never fully satisfied with a cheap imitation, neither do we realize how badly we have been misled.

It is here that the connection between Nazi Germany and the rest of the human race becomes painfully clear. We are all *glory junkies*, with the pursuit of significance often leading us down dark and dismal paths. In this, the distance between evil and our natural quest for human validation is much shorter than we realize.

The Christian life is about more than a burdensome list of obligations, or even a far-off destiny. Through the person of Jesus Christ, we can establish an ever-present *identity,* magnificent beyond all natural capacity. Our Creator calls us upward, to an unflappable sense of significance that can never be entirely at home on this earthen sphere. When that magnificence becomes rooted in our inner person, it is only a matter of time until we naturally broadcast it through our outward actions.

QUESTIONS

1. What similarities are common to all humanity?

2. What evidence do we have that all people crave significance?

3. Why does human glory pale in comparison to God's magnificence?

FURTHER READING: Genesis 1:26–31 and Psalm 49

PRAYER: Dear God, please open my eyes to true glory!

DAY TWO
MORE THAN AN OPINION

———◦———

Yours, Lord, is the greatness and the power and the glory and the splendor and the majesty, for everything in the heavens and on earth belongs to You. Yours, Lord, is the kingdom, and You are exalted as head over all.

1 Chronicles 29:11 (HCSB)

Man is never sufficiently touched and affected by the awareness of his lowly state until he has compared himself with God's majesty.
—John Calvin

In any sport, few achievements compare to the glory of winning a world championship. I know because I live near Pittsburgh, Pennsylvania—home of the Penguins (hockey), Pirates (baseball), and Steelers (American football). Each team has won multiple championships, and it is not uncommon for upwards of five hundred thousand people to crowd the city streets in a celebratory parade.

With such a rich sports tradition, Pittsburgh understandably boasts a long history of athletic wonders. Of those great players, one name routinely resurfaces, even though he retired from Major League Baseball in 1917 and passed on from this world in 1955. That name is Honus Wagner—otherwise known as "The Flying Dutchman."

> And it also turns out that while Honus was the best third baseman in the league, he was also the best first baseman, the best second baseman, the best shortstop, and the best outfielder. That was in fielding. And since he led the league in batting eight times between 1900 and 1911, you know that he was the best hitter, too. As well as the best base runner.[1]

---
1. Lawrence S. Ritter, *The Glory of Their Times*, new enl. ed. (New York: William Morrow and Company, 1966), 23.

It was not his success on the baseball diamond that now casts the spotlight back onto Wagner, but the value of his T206 baseball card. Issued by the American Tobacco Company between 1909 and 1911, that card is one of the rarest and most expensive in the world. As a player, the most Wagner ever earned in a year was $10,000. But if you want to buy a T206 Wagner baseball card, it will likely cost you several million dollars.

A ballplayer's glory effectively promoted cigarette sales. The image of a professional player on one side of a card elicited the wonder of young boys while cigarette advertisements on the other side enticed their desires. For reasons unclear, Wagner would have none of it. And by withholding permission, he forced the tobacco company to suspend production. Less than 200 were produced, making the baseball artifact exceedingly rare—and thus valuable.

What makes a piece of printed cardboard less than four by seven centimeters worth an absurd amount of money? A combination of fame and rarity might seem to be the obvious answer, but in reality, its value is based on nothing more than *human opinion*. A baseball card, after all, is only worth what someone is willing to pay for it. Such a quandary this realization creates!

Seeking to discern true glory from a feeble substitute compels us to develop a keen eye for value, to become expert investigators, if you will. Whether we speak of collecting sports memorabilia, wine, or antiques, appealing counterfeits abound. I am alluding, however, to something on a far grander scale. Our quest for real significance begins by ascertaining the difference between fleeting human glory and the eternal glory of God. This effort requires that we also explore the disparity between people's opinions and inherent greatness.

Toward the end of World War II, two infuriated Nazi field marshals sent a teletype to members of the armed forces describing the court-martial and execution of several officers who failed to meet their expectations. The memo ended by stating, "Who does not live in honor will die in shame."[2] History tells us that their opinions of honor and shame were painfully distorted.

The Hebrew word for glory most prevalent in Old Testament writings, *kabod*, generally involves a sense of *weightiness*:

---

2. Ken Hechler, *The Bridge at Remagen* (New York: Ballantine Books, 1957), 212.

The basic meaning is "to be heavy, weighty," a meaning which is only rarely used literally, the figurative... being more common. From this figurative usage it is an easy step to the concept of a "weighty" person in society, someone who is honorable, impressive, worthy of respect.[3]

Ancient Hebrews often used *kabod* to describe the sense of honor conferred upon a person because of his or her significance in society. However, in the Old Testament, *kabod* can also mean a manifestation of God's splendor. Thus, the ancients sometimes experienced the manifestation of God's glory, but also gave Him glory as they recognized the weightiness of His magnificent splendor.

In the *Septuagint*—a Greek translation of the Jewish Bible—the word predominately used to translate the Hebrew concept of glory is *doxa*. The Biblical Greek meaning of *doxa*, however, strays from that of common usage. In the secular realm, *doxa* was mainly a matter of thought and opinion, but in Jewish (and Christian) religious thought, "it denotes 'divine and heavenly radiance,' the 'loftiness and majesty' of God, and even the 'being of God' and His world."[4]

I highlight the difference between the secular and spiritual use of *doxa* to paint a poignant picture for us all. Jewish scholars took a secular concept and applied their own definition because they viewed God as uniquely and self-sufficiently majestic apart from human opinion. These men who drew from a rich religious lineage understood that our human ideas of glory pale when compared to revealed manifestations of the Almighty.

Glory, in many ways, is intimately linked to power and ability. People idolized Honus Wagner because his athletic prowess on the baseball diamond surpassed all others in his day. But what human possesses abilities that were not first given by God? Furthermore, with human glory, that ability must be one that is admired and valued by those who have the means to influence public sentiment.

A rare baseball card needs the opinion of wealthy investors to maintain its value. If the economy were to crash, you can be sure that

---
3. John N. Oswalt, "943 כבד," ed. R. Laird Harris, Gleason L. Archer Jr., and Bruce K. Waltke, *Theological Wordbook of the Old Testament* (Chicago: Moody Press, 1999), 426.
4. Gerhard Kittel, Geoffrey W. Bromiley, and Gerhard Friedrich, eds., *Theological Dictionary of the New Testament* (Grand Rapids, MI: Eerdmans, 1964), 237.

the value of all Honus Wagner T206 cards would drop precipitously. In contrast, the sovereign King of Glory needs nothing to affirm His significance. Divine splendor does not increase or diminish based on the rise and fall of an opinion-driven stock market. In other words, *our Creator's glory has nothing to do with what we think and everything to do with true substance.*

If our assessment of God does nothing to affect majestic glory, does it even matter what we think? Absolutely! Strange as it may seem to some, how we perceive God—along with how we think He perceives us—has far-reaching ramifications. What we think, say, and do in our universal search for significance profoundly influences our well-being both now and for eternity. The truly wise person— one who sees beyond the jubilation of short-lived opinions—will both speak and live with such a reality in mind.

When we as humans choose to give God glory through praise, worship, and giving thanks, we are not adding worth to the Creator of heaven and earth. We are aligning with an eternal reality that cannot be otherwise. The One who created the cosmos in all its greatness far surpasses its splendor and magnificence.

The apostle Paul wrote that our Creator "alone possesses immortality and dwells in unapproachable light" (1 Timothy 6:16). Such incomprehensible glory requires further exploration, an effort we will begin to undertake in our next reading.

QUESTIONS

1. How is glory connected to "weightiness" in society?

2. How do glory and ability relate to one another?

3. What are the implications of depending on human popularity rather than on God's opinion to determine our sense of value?

FURTHER READING: Psalm 147:1–11; Isaiah 40:12–26; and 1 Corinthians 4:6–7

PRAYER: Lord, please help me to focus on Your greatness instead of fleeting human glory.

DAY THREE
THE KING OF GLORY

Who is this King of glory?
The LORD of hosts,
He is the King of glory.

Psalm 24:10

When Jesus came the first time, He suffered in shame. The second time, He will reign in glory. The first time, they crowned Him with thorns. The second time, He will wear a crown of glory... The first time, He came in the greatest humility, riding on a donkey. The second time, He's coming in power and glory. The first time, He was rejected of men. The second time, every knee shall bow. Even the knee of every unbeliever will bow and confess that Jesus Christ is Lord, to the glory of God the Father.

—Adrian Rogers

In the USA, he was known as "the King," or more fully stated, "the King of Rock 'n' Roll." I refer, of course, to the music legend Elvis Presley. Famed composer Leonard Bernstein once called Elvis "the greatest cultural force in the twentieth century." Presley influenced Western culture like no other musician, paving the way not only for future performers, but also an entirely new mindset. Even the Christian church has been deeply affected, as evidenced by the fast-paced, beat-driven worship music used in a vast number of churches. The organ, once a staple of almost every Western church, is in many ways dead, and Elvis is the killer.

Elvis Presley himself died at the young age of forty-two from heart failure brought on by prescription drug overuse. When it comes to human stardom, Presley was a cultural king, but in light of eternity, his time spent on this planet amounted to little more than a momentary blip on the radar screen of human history. Furthermore,

Presley's never-ending quest for approval created an emotional roller coaster, which in turn increased his susceptibility to drug abuse.

The words of American Idol contestant Chris Daughtry about the rock 'n' roll king reveal an additional dynamic of human fame:

> "I can't compare myself to Elvis, not even a little bit. People put you on a pedestal; it almost feels like you're being worshiped sometimes which is not normal for a human being to deal with, not even a little."[1]

The Bible also speaks of a King who is widely worshipped—the King of Glory—and His influence on this world remains unrivaled. Whereas human history has seen untold numbers of kings and lords rise and fall, He is *the King of kings and Lord of lords*. Of all the kings who have reigned on this earth, He is the greatest. Of all the lords who have commanded others to do their bidding, He is the most powerful.

Jesus is the Alpha and Omega, the beginning and the end (Revelation 1:8). He is also the author of creation (Colossians 1:16). He brought all things into being, and nothing came into existence apart from Him (John 1:3). The King of Glory reigns over all, and He will one day bring wise recompense to every unjust act. Even as Christ's kingdom stands supreme for all eternity, the loftiness of our human governments will crumble into nothing but vague and distant memories.

His is the name above all names, meaning that no ruler, power, or authority can begin to compare (Ephesians 1:19b–21). All who sit as judges over human behavior will one day be subject to the judgment of Him whose throne is established upon righteousness and justice. Speechless, every opposing voice will fall silent when the Son of God reveals His full glory and splendor. Every knee will bow to His sovereign authority, and every tongue will confess the universal reality of His lordship (Philippians 2:9–11).

Psalm 24:10 also speaks of "the Lord of Hosts"—the self-existing God who reigns over all (see also 1 Samuel 1:3). *Hosts* in the Old

---

1. "Quotes About Elvis," Elvis Presley Enterprises, accessed April 2, 2024, https://www.graceland.com/quotes-about-elvis.

Testament can refer to a mighty army, the angelic host, or the sun, moon, and stars (i.e., all of creation). Whatever interpretation the authors had in mind when they penned "hosts" is irrelevant because they all apply to God. *He is the Lord over everything.*

Imagine, if you will, the glory of a single star up close. Even the greatest among us are dwarfed by its immensity and blinded by its brightness. Now, try to comprehend a hundred billion galaxies with a hundred billion stars in each. The Lord of Hosts created it all with but a few spoken words! It is no wonder that heaven's angels live to obey His will and proclaim His glory.

God is the "rock star" of the cosmos, rendering all others mere pretenders. *All glory apart from His is received as a gift of creation.* Angels, for example, are amazing, brilliant beings (Revelation 18:1). Remove them from the King of Glory's presence, however, and they go dark. That is what happened to the devil. Once clothed in magnificence, Lucifer was the "star of the morning" (Isaiah 14:12). Now, he crawls about on his belly eating our dust, impotent and unable to recover his former glory (Genesis 3:14).

How are these ideas relevant to us as individuals? The human heart craves glory—a self-evident reality that is displayed in virtually every arena of life. Government leaders boast luxurious lifestyles, sports stadiums pack to the brim with starstruck fans, even a young child shouts, "Look at me! Look at me!" We consider these and many more glory-driven tendencies to be normal aspects of everyday life.

Sadly, our pursuit of glory independent from God continues to create problems of epic proportions. In thinking ourselves to be wise and superior, we have become hapless fools. There is but one King of Glory, and only by aligning ourselves with His reality can we move away from the sociological dysfunctions that plague the human race.

If we do not wisely learn to draw from our connection with the King of Glory, the vain pursuit of significance will dominate and corrupt our short existence in this world. Do you doubt me on this? Take a little time to study human history and the chaos that has resulted from self-exaltation. Heartbreaking evidence of dysfunction abounds.

The apostle Paul instructed his readers to "do nothing from selfishness or empty conceit" (Philippians 2:3). The Greek word (*kenodoxia*) translated as "empty conceit" means "vainglory." Human glory is nothing more than *pseudo-glory*. Every magnificent specimen of human flesh will one day decay and emit a repulsive stench. What does that say about our greatness? Even so, breaking free from a compulsive pursuit of significance is no small feat. True liberty can indeed be gained, but not apart from inviting the King of kings and Lord of lords to actively work in our hearts.

Charting a course for true glory propels us on a journey fraught with difficulty. We might compare the experience to trying to enter a football stadium just as the crowd is exiting after a nail-biting championship game. It would be a fool's errand for a loser late to the party—or so it seems. While the world revels in pseudo-significance, Christians appear to be missing all the fun.

Migrating from being enamored with human approval to receiving divine glory is not for the faint of heart. Many of us have invested so much in our pursuit of significance that we are unwilling to let it go, to admit our wrong, to surrender as worthless that which has consumed our life's energy. *If we genuinely seek the significance that flows from heaven's throne, we must learn to spurn the vain desire for loftiness that has enamored and captivated the human race throughout the centuries.* Forfeiting human glory for the divine will turn our lives inside out—but in a beautifully transformational way! The true King of Glory would not have it any other way!

QUESTIONS

1. What are some of the ramifications of Jesus being the King of kings and the Lord of lords?

2. Why do both angels and humans "go dark" when separated from God's glory?

3. What are some of the methods we use to pursue human glory?

FURTHER READING: Philippians 2:3–11 and Revelation 19:11–16

PRAYER: King of Glory, please give me strength and courage to stay on the path of unfading glory.

DAY FOUR
THE GLORY OF HIS PRESENCE

―――――――◆◆◆―――――――

So Jesus, knowing all the things that were coming upon Him, went forth and said to them, "Whom do you seek?" They answered Him, "Jesus the Nazarene." He said to them, "I am He." And Judas also, who was betraying Him, was standing with them. So when He said to them, "I am He," they drew back and fell to the ground.

John 18:4–6

I had an overwhelming experience of the Lord's presence. I felt so powerfully overcome by the nearness of the Holy Spirit that I had to ask the Lord to draw back lest He kill me. It was so glorious that I couldn't stand more than a small portion of it.
—Mordecai Ham

Ancient Rome employed crucifixion as one of the most inglorious punishments conceived by humankind. The wooden cross not only tortured and killed the body but also the soul. Indeed, they designed the entire experience to publicly shame the poor wretch. Observers looked on in horror at the bloody, shameful mess of crucified flesh, gravely aware that Roman authority was not to be challenged.

From the perspective of His Jewish peers, Christ's crucifixion marked the depths of humiliation—an aspiring messiah abandoned by a holy God, his visions of grandeur scattered into oblivion under the thumb of a pagan nation. From an eternal viewpoint, however, the cross unveiled Jesus' selfless glory in a most majestic fashion.

Humanity momentarily gasps in admiration when truly selfless glory comes to light, but strikingly few of us embrace such other-centeredness as a way of life. We all admire the likes of Mother Theresa, for example, but pitifully few follow in her lowly footsteps. Jesus went lower still.

Christ's death and resurrection marked more than one amazing feat. Rising from the depths of the grave is an obvious triumph, but Jesus also scored a vital and necessary victory when He willingly chose to endure the shame of the cross and its painful tortures at the hands of those who owed Him allegiance. Herein, we find ample evidence that *King of Glory* is a title aptly deserved.

The weight of His coming fate bore so heavily on Jesus' heart that "His sweat became like drops of blood" as He wept and prayed in the garden of Gethsemane (Luke 22:39–46). Emotionally alone, His slumbering friends failing Him miserably, Jesus cried out, "Father, if You are willing, remove this cup from Me; yet not My will, but Yours be done."

Christ's prayer in Gethsemane is beyond profound, reflecting a powerful act of alignment. Living the life of a flesh-clad human, Jesus did what no man or woman had ever accomplished; He fully yielded His will to the heavenly Father's—and did so amidst the worst imaginable circumstances, no less. What Adam and Eve failed to do in the garden of Eden (Genesis 3:1–6), the Son of Man courageously accomplished in the garden of Gethsemane.

When the mindsets of our planet align with heaven, something amazing begins to happen: *heaven comes to earth*. In this particular case, that convergence brought about a weighty manifestation of God's presence, which moves us toward an often-ignored aspect of Christ's arrest.

Just as the Son of God finished fully surrendering His will to the heavenly Father's, the soft glow of torches illuminated the night sky (John 18:3). Guided by Judas the traitor, a cohort (600 men) of armed soldiers approached Jesus and His small band of disciples, who suddenly found themselves fully awake. Well aware of the unfathomable pain about to come upon Him, humanity's Savior sought to protect those the Father had put under His charge.

Boldly stepping forward when all others would cower, Jesus asked, "Whom do you seek?" Unnerved by His confidence, the delegation answered, "Jesus of Nazareth." How did Christ respond? "I am He."[1] What happened next is a scene worthy of legends.

---

1. The Greek text does not include the pronoun "He," so it is entirely possible that Jesus was at this time proclaiming His deity by saying, "I am." (See Exodus 3:14.)

Even as the words left Christ's mouth, over 600 armed and well-trained military men "drew back and fell to the ground." What would cause such an inconceivable reaction by this group of battle-hardened warriors? Was it the profound nature of His words? Not likely. How about His bold confidence? I do not think so. While certainly worthy of admiration, something more than courage elicited such an unusual response.

What, then, brought those men to their faces? The weight of the divine presence! Because Christ displayed ultimate glory by embracing the humiliation of the cross for the sake of others, the glory of God inexplicably manifested for a brief moment on a tiny piece of earthly real estate.

Such an explanation is entirely reasonable in light of Biblical history. The Scriptures teach that God's presence is everywhere, but that on occasion, the glory of His presence manifests for humans to see and experience. Those moments, you can be sure, overwhelm even the most brazen of souls.

The divine presence set Israel apart from all other nations. From the time that the oppressed Israelites left the glorious cities of Egypt, God's manifested glory stayed near (Exodus 13:17–22). Then, while in the wilderness, they constructed the Ark of the Covenant as a place for His presence to dwell, as well as a portable tabernacle (tent) to house the Ark (Exodus 25–27).

> Then the cloud covered the tent of meeting, and the glory of the Lord filled the tabernacle. Moses was not able to enter the tent of meeting because the cloud had settled on it, and the glory of the Lord filled the tabernacle. Exodus 40:34–35

Later, after years of labor and untold resources, King Solomon's workers completed the building of a temple to house God's presence among His people. Guided by his father David's example, Solomon also commissioned a priestly choir to praise and worship God with singing accompanied by a variety of instruments.

The Ark of the Covenant, which could not be touched and had been carried from place to place with poles, was at last coming to a "permanent" home among God's covenant people. As the priests carried the Ark into the temple, filling its halls with enthusiastic praise, God's presence manifested so strongly that they could no longer stand under the weight of His glory.

> It happened that when the priests came from the holy place, the cloud filled the house of the Lord, so that the priests could not stand to minister because of the cloud, for the glory of the Lord filled the house of the Lord. 1 Kings 8:10–11

Yet another expression of God's glorious presence played a pivotal role in the apostle Paul's conversion experience. Though convinced of his own "superior" beliefs, the young man was apprehended by a heavenly glory that exposed the depths of his ignorance (Acts 9:1–19). No matter how hard we try to limit Christianity to the realm of the intellect, we can never contain our Creator's fullness. The mysterious glory of God puts even our best arguments to shame.

From the experience of Adam and Eve in the garden of Eden, to eternal glory in heaven—and everything in between—the true substance of life has always been intricately tied to the presence of our Creator. Apart from that presence, an enduring sense of personal significance will always be lacking. Whether we fall to our knees at His majesty, or simply rest in His quiet peace, enduring glory is to be found only in His nearness.

QUESTIONS

1. How does true glory relate to selfless love?

2. Why was the contrast between Jesus on the throne of heaven and Jesus on the cross so extreme?

3. What is the danger of making Christianity simply a religion of the intellect while ignoring the pursuit of God's presence?

FURTHER READING: 2 Chronicles 5:11–14 and John 18:1–11

PRAYER: Dear Lord, please give me both an understanding of Your ways and the realization of Your presence.

DAY FIVE
THE ULTIMATE TEMPTATION

"For God knows that in the day you eat from it your eyes will be opened, and you will be like God, knowing good and evil."
                                                                Genesis 3:5

The essence of temptation is the invitation to live independently of God.
                                                                —Neil T. Anderson

I remember a time in high school when a classmate and I stood waiting in line to enter the auditorium. As we talked, we noticed a couple of bare wires protruding from an uncovered electrical box. "What," we asked each other, "are the chances of a public school allowing two electrically charged wires to be so easily accessible to a building full of teenagers?" Subsequently, my classmate dared me to grab both wires. And so I did. They were alive with electricity!

Thankfully, the amount of electrical charge I felt was minimal. Had the circumstances been different, however, I might not have lived to tell the story of my own foolishness. Perhaps it was that experience that led to a little quip I jokingly embraced while in college: "I can resist anything but temptation!"

Temptation knocks on our door daily, if not moment by moment. Always, it entices us to actions that are unhealthy, unwise, wrong, or immoral. By its very nature, temptation appeals to our basic human desires: curiosity, appetite, and ego, to name a few. Some temptations appear to carry minimal consequences, but they can hasten the day of death nonetheless. Rarely do temptations come out of nowhere; instead, a "tempter" often entices us to make regrettable choices.

The Bible identifies the tempter of all tempters as *Satan*, or the lord of temptation, if you will. This fallen angel, who continually seeks to steal, kill, and destroy, preys upon our natural tendencies in an effort to separate us from God's glorious presence. Though we might be tempted to laugh off the existence of the devil, his dastardly schemes poison our collective human experience.

Two prophetic passages from the Old Testament—Isaiah 14:3-23 and Ezekiel 28:1-19—speak both of earthly kings and an amazing angelic being, whose name the Latin language translates as "Lucifer." Created by God with exquisite beauty, Lucifer became enamored both with himself and the majesty of God's throne. Blinded by his desire for glory, he recruited a third of the angels and staged an attempted coup in a violent but vain effort to depose the King of Glory.

From these prophetic passages, we might establish Lucifer's mantra as, "I will ascend to heaven's throne and become God!" Or more simply put, "I will ascend!" I find this simple, short statement to be profoundly significant for the human race as well. *An innate desire to ascend to the highest place of power and glory affects virtually every arena of our existence.*

The appeal of glory captivates our attention and blinds us to the reality around us. Indeed, Lucifer's seismic error resulted from losing sight of the fact that he had no glory within himself apart from his Creator. *No divine presence, no glory; this is our universal reality.*

The good news is that Lucifer and his lackeys were effortlessly thrown from heaven. In an instant, the most majestic of all the angels became the inglorious devil, slithering about, consumed by dark and violent thoughts, hating all that is good with every hiss-filled breath. The bad news is that they landed where we live: on earth. What suffering has resulted!

It was the fallen Lucifer who took the form of a wily serpent (see Revelation 12:9) in the garden paradise of Eden (Genesis 3:1-6). He then tempted Adam and Eve to disobey their Creator by enticing them with the same desire that caused his own fall. The "ultimate temptation" to be like God has ensnared humanity ever since that fateful moment. "You will be like God," or reading between the lines just a little, "You will be like God apart from God," has been the driving force of human dysfunction since the beginning of our time.

From the core of these ill-spoken words radiated the appeal of *independent glory*. In other words, Adam and Eve were tempted to believe that if they ate from the tree of the knowledge of good and evil, they would have glory within themselves apart from their Creator. This description might not fit our traditional understanding of sin, but in so many ways, this pursuit of independent glory forms the foundation of human sinfulness.

In the apostle Paul's letter to the Romans, we find a significant nuance of Scripture that is routinely overlooked:

> For all have sinned and fall short of the glory of God. Romans 3:23

Notice that Paul added "and fall short of the glory of God" rather than simply saying that "all have sinned." At the heart of sin is the quest, yes, even compulsion, to attain divine glory apart from God.

The Greek word *hamartano*, translated as "sin" in Romans 3:23, can mean "to miss the mark," as an archer might miss a target.[1] God's glory is the bulls-eye that all humanity seeks to hit, but even the greatest among us fall woefully short. Society's elite will shoot their arrows farther than those who are ordinary, but it matters little; not a single one will land anywhere near the target.

Consider the implications! Seeking glory is embodied in our ever-present quest to find a significant identity. All the sin, death, and destruction that plague humanity are rooted in the lie, "you will be like God apart from God." This means the powers of darkness used—and continue to use—the promise of an elevated identity, disassociated from God, as the ultimate temptation to enslave us.

If the quest for glory presents the ultimate temptation, we are inclined to think that the Christian gospel is an *identity message*. When I first began exploring how to stand strong against the temptations of sin, only a few Christian leaders emphasized the importance of identity. Now, this truth is taking root. The church is finally realizing the necessity of establishing our identity as sons and daughters of the King of Glory. The need for a secure identity in Christ is a message for our age and one that we dare not take lightly.

Many of us have been heartbroken and mired in various forms of destructive behavior. We try in vain to craft positive self-images, instead finding ourselves feeling condemned, confused, and worthless. Both the hard and soft sciences offer solutions to our

---

[1] James Strong, Enhanced Strong's Lexicon (Woodside Bible Fellowship, 1995).

struggles, yet nothing seems to free us from the endless quest for significance. Mere religion is no help either. *If we think that pleasing God requires attaining to religious or moral standards, we will only intensify our struggles.*

I have known sincere people to walk away from their Creator because they could not break free from habitual sins. Those struggling souls felt that disassociating themselves from the loving King of Glory somehow "liberated" them from the need to "measure up," when nothing could be further from the truth. The long-term consequences of such a decision far outweigh the benefits of any temporary relief. Furthermore, God knew that we could never meet His perfect standards, and so He designed the Christian gospel with the burden of perfection falling upon Christ and not us.

Jesus is our source of liberation, and hope lies not in running from God, but in drawing nearer. Those who wish to break free from the bonds of sin and live in victory over its dominion, do so not through mere self-discovery, but by discovering themselves as sons and daughters of the King of kings and Lord of lords. Our Creator desires that we be free, and true freedom can be found only in Him.

Transitioning from the pursuit of human glory to receiving the glory given by God encompasses far more than feeling better about ourselves. It is a journey toward liberty, victory, and hope for a meaningful future. But for freedom to be realized, we must first understand and overcome the ultimate temptation: the desire to be God and independently attain His glory.

QUESTIONS

1. What is the *ultimate temptation*?

2. Give an example of how the pursuit of glory blinds people.

3. What is the relationship between identity and glory?

FURTHER READING: Genesis 3:1–7 and Hebrews 4:12–16

PRAYER: Lord, please deliver me from the universal human temptation to live independent from You.

DAY SIX
NAKED AND ASHAMED

I advise you to buy from Me gold refined by fire so that you may become rich, and white garments so that you may clothe yourself, and that the shame of your nakedness will not be revealed; and eye salve to anoint your eyes so that you may see.
Revelation 3:18

Unless Christianity is wholly false, the perception of ourselves which we have in moments of shame must be the only true one.
—C.S. Lewis

Have you ever fabricated a lie to avoid embarrassment? During my brief stint as a church youth leader, I worked with a young man who told our group that he had shot a turkey with an arrow. His sister, who was also present, immediately contested his story. "You don't even have a bow!" she blurted out for all to hear. Terrified of looking bad in front of his peers, the boy proceeded to craft a series of falsehoods in a vain attempt to cover himself. His efforts were less than successful.

This young man blatantly lied, but he is by no means alone. Practically all of us have told lies or fabricated stories to protect and advance our images. I know that I have, and more than once! Why are so many of us prone to such "untruths"? In large part, it is because we fear the pain of ridicule that results from our true selves being exposed.

The King of Glory never intended us to live in constant fear of exposure and ridicule. Only after Adam and Eve succumbed to the ultimate temptation did such unrest ravage our peace. Genesis 2 tells the story of human creation in the garden of Eden—a lush paradise that we wish represented our everyday experience. The chapter ends with an intriguing statement:

> And the man and his wife were both naked and were not ashamed. Genesis 2:25

Although fully exposed, the father and mother of civilization felt no sense of embarrassment. And just as importantly, they had no fear of vulnerability, exposure, harassment, or exploitation. *Munch. Munch.* It took only a couple of bites of the forbidden fruit for their innocent, safe world to come crashing down. In an instant, the father and mother of humanity recoiled in fear and shame.

A person does not need a doctorate in theology to discern that no changes in their outward physical state had transpired from Genesis 2:25 to Genesis 3:7. Instead, their sudden ability to "see" brought about the most intense reactions: fear, blame, and a desperate need to cover themselves.

Their eyes being opened meant that they suddenly became aware. This sense of awareness then opened the floodgates of shame.

- Shame for having disobeyed God
- Shame for having been duped by the evil serpent
- Shame for destroying the pristine beauty of creation
- Shame for taking on the heinous nature of the serpent
- Shame for failing to measure up to newly realized standards of divine perfection
- Shame for forfeiting the glory that once clothed them

The Hebrew word for shame, *bôš*, primarily means, "to fall into disgrace, normally through failure, either of self or of an object of trust."[1] Furthermore, this idea of shame is closely akin to public humiliation "in that the English stresses the inner attitude, the state of mind, while the Hebrew means 'to come to shame' and stresses the sense of public disgrace, a physical state."[2] We can rightly compare the contrast between glory and shame to that between the noonday sun and the deepest night.

---

1. John N. Oswalt, "222 בּוֹשׁ," ed. R. Laird Harris, Gleason L. Archer Jr., and Bruce K. Waltke, *Theological Wordbook of the Old Testament* (Chicago: Moody Press, 1999), 97.
2. Ibid.

Whereas God created humanity in His image and wired for glory, shame communicates a forlorn sense of humiliation due to a perceived lack of glory. *Shame broadcasts our flawed state, not just for what we have done, but for who we are.* "I will ascend!" quickly became, "Oh no, I have descended!" Adam and Eve had been created in and for glory, but their willful disobedience produced the opposite of its intended effect; they became glory deficient.

People need glory (i.e., a sense of significance) to thrive emotionally. Where there is no glory, life will be miserable and vitality lacking. Adam and Eve felt such intense feelings of shame that they labored to cover themselves with the abrasive leaves of a fig tree. Then, when their Creator drew near, the two cowered in fear and began casting blame. Rather than celebrating newfound independence, humans had become dependent on the fragile leaves of a tree to cover their naked vulnerability and protect themselves from exploitation. They did the best they could with what they had, but can you imagine fig leaves being sold in a clothing store?

In His mercy, the Lord killed innocent animals and used their skins to clothe His wayward children. God could have said, "You are fine naked. There is no need for you to cover yourselves," but He did not. Furthermore, our Creator spilled the blood of innocent animals He had created not long prior. Clearly, God agreed with Adam and Eve that they needed to be clothed.

There is nothing inherently shameful about the human body; it presents a magnificent display of our Creator's handiwork. However, the original sin of Eden mysteriously knitted sinful desires to human flesh. Covering our intimate places in public provides a powerful and necessary reminder that an inherently sinful nature, combined with the lack of true glory, makes us "spiritually naked" before God. It is because of this connection that the Bible almost always portrays nakedness in a negative light.

It should be no surprise that human self-glorification and the celebration of public nudity often go hand in hand. But when we foolishly violate God-given boundaries and proclaim our personal right to do as we please, our selfish pride becomes our spiritual shame. The one person we do not want to be shamed by is God, but that will be the tragic fate of those who persist in their own way.

Our dysfunction runs deeper still. In addition to shame, humanity's first act of disobedience also released a torrent of guilt and condemnation. I define guilt as "the nagging burden resulting from the failure to meet a moral standard," while I see condemnation as "the hammering voice of judgment that constantly berates us over our failure to measure up."

Shame, guilt, and condemnation are "comrades of misery" that force their way into human hearts and become permanent squatters. Each feeling harasses us in its own demeaning way. Guilt proclaims our failure to meet a moral standard, shame poisons our psyche, and condemnation beats us to an emotional pulp.

The Lord wants to free us from shame because it is such a painful and powerful emotion that simply the fear of being shamed can be used to torment and manipulate us like puppets on a string. How terrified we are of public humiliation!

Are you in need of good news? Jesus lowered Himself to the deepest depths of shame and humiliation so He could banish the comrades of misery into exile. *Regardless of what we experience in this cruel and chaotic world, fully embracing the gospel of Jesus Christ guarantees every child of God a shame-free eternity.* The clothing of His resplendent glory will forever bury our spiritual nakedness, which is never to be seen again. Drawing closer to Jesus means moving further from the toxic misery of shame and fear.

QUESTIONS

1. Can you think of a humorous story about a lie you once told to avoid embarrassment?

2. How does the fear of shame subject us to manipulation and control?

3. Discuss what life would be like with no fear of shame.

FURTHER READING: Isaiah 49:22–26 and Joel 2:21–27

PRAYER: Good God, thank You that shame, guilt, and condemnation are not a part of Your plan for me. Please help me to know Your truth so that I can be forever free from these comrades of misery!

DAY SEVEN
FIG LEAVES

Then the eyes of both of them were opened, and they knew that they were naked; and they sewed fig leaves together and made themselves loin coverings.

Genesis 3:7

We break our backs to keep up our fronts.

—Unknown

I cannot begin to imagine the overwhelming sense of shame that Adam and Eve felt after eating the forbidden fruit. Having foolishly forfeited the majestic glory of God, they now stood exposed and vulnerable, terrified of what might happen next. Their solution? Fig leaves!

We know nothing about how they did it, but our first parents vainly labored to cover their nakedness with the green, leafy appendages of a fig tree. Then, when their Creator drew near for His evening stroll, they scurried into the trees to play an unhappy game of hide and seek.

> "Where are you?... Who told you that you were naked? Have you eaten from the tree of which I commanded you not to eat?"
> Genesis 3:9–11

The Creator of all things does not ask questions because He lacks information. Instead, the Lord made pointed queries to bring His wayward children face-to-face with the error of their ways. Sadly, they preferred perpetuating the error over the pain of having their darkness exposed by God's resplendent light.

In essence, this was the birth of our human version of glory. Rather than resting peacefully in the substance of a real, God-given identity, our first parents presented an outward "fig-leaf image" to cover their disgrace and cast themselves in a more favorable light. People have been wearing masks and cloaks ever since.

Just as humanity's glory deficiency continues in modern times, so does our manic use of fig leaves to mask our deficiencies—*fig-leaf mania*, if you will. Carefully, we craft images to clothe ourselves with favor in the eyes of our peers. The fig leaves of Eden more or less symbolize the figurative types of leaves we attempt to cover—or is it embellish?—ourselves with today:

> **1. Performance** – how well we perfect certain skills compared to other people. The range of performance-based approval runs the gamut from vocation to music to athletics to parenting to religious observation and beyond. No arena of life is exempt.
>
> **2. Appearance** – how we look in light of cultural standards. The standards change with history and geography, but the core idea stays the same. People seek validation through physical beauty, by having the "appropriate" body shape, being of a certain skin color, and of course, wearing the expected fashions of the day.
>
> **3. Possessions** – the size of our income and the extent of our accumulated goods. Whether we speak of land ownership, cows in a field, or pricey cars, the more we have, the higher we climb the ladder of significance—or so we try to convince ourselves.
>
> **4. Status** – the significance we draw from positions of power, influence, and advantage. Elite social status, envious titles, and high positions of authority shout to the world, "I am ***somebody!***"
>
> **5. Knowledge** – what and how much we know compared to those around us. Possessing more knowledge, along with greater mental capacity, makes us feel superior to those "common folk" who fail to meet our intellectual standards.
>
> **6. Association with others** – finding a sense of significance by connecting with those deemed to be weighty in society. People who lack significance of their own will often "hijack" fig-leaf glory from athletes, movie stars, and other notable celebrities.

The wearing of splendidly adorned fig leaves, we are led to believe, is where true greatness lies. Stronger, higher, shinier, wealthier, and more powerful are all seen as marks of individual or group superiority. But what if they are wrong? What if our standards of greatness fabricate only a deceptive facade? What if true greatness exposes our fig leaves as little more than ragged and dirty laundry?

Gaze intently upon our worldly pursuit of human glory, and before long you will see gaping holes in our fig-leaf philosophy:

1. Human glory creates a false sense of superiority. What do we have that we have not been given? Ability and success are gifts of God. We can work to improve our skills but only by developing abilities already imparted by our Creator.

2. Human glory creates a false sense of confidence. Our bodies are subject to forces beyond our control. Some of us exhibit great strength and endurance compared to others, but any one of us is only a heartbeat from death. All it takes is a significant illness or near tragedy to bring our arrogant selves back to earth.

3. Human standards are fickle and easily manipulated. Small groups of people with the expertise to shape public opinion can manipulate and control a society by manipulating and controlling cultural standards. Contemporary fashion provides a typical example. Need I say more?

4. There is no clarity regarding whose standards we are compelled to meet. In high school, we all vied for popularity by trying to meet standards of appearance and ability. There were no clear specifications, however, about what standards mattered and who decided them. How was I to know that my bowling and dart throwing abilities would fail to land me dates with the popular girls?

5. The pursuit of self-achieved glory puts upon our shoulders an impossible burden of perfection. It is not simply a favorable image that human glory demands, but a flawless portrait of perfection. When we seek to be like God apart from God, perfection becomes our overarching standard.

6. **Clothing ourselves in human glory stratifies society and divides people.** When we exalt and idolize certain body shapes, skin colors, or ethnic backgrounds, we instantly put ourselves at odds with those who are unlike us. The vast amount of conflict in our world is, at its roots, a glory issue.

7. **All glory—apart from that which God possesses in Himself—eventually fades.** Smooth, supple skin turns to leather-like wrinkles. Lion-like athletic prowess ends with using a cane to shuffle slowly along. We want to live but dread growing old. Why are there so few options? In the end, time is no friend to human glory.

Fig-leaf mania—it is the human way. Regardless of the outward images we portray, deep inside we fear that something is amiss. Living in a shallow world where image is everything cannot help but leave the true substance of life severely lacking. Thus, we dread times of quiet, because it is when the glitter fades and the noise subsides that the shallow reality of our existence becomes evident.

Times of quiet, however, are what we need. If, in hope, we bring the pain of our current reality to God, our heartfelt prayers will lead us to the throne of the King of Glory. Not only is He willing and able to heal past hurts, He also seeks to satisfy our glory deficiencies with the imperishable substance of eternal significance.

QUESTIONS

1. In what ways does human glory create a false sense of superiority?

2. Why is perfection the standard for those who seek to be validated by self-achieved glory?

3. How does the pursuit of human glory serve to stratify society and divide people?

FURTHER READING: Philippians 3 and Revelation 3:14–22

PRAYER: Dear God, please clothe me with Your glory so that I can break free from the fig-leaf mentality driving this world.

DAY EIGHT
THE DAY OF ICHABOD

And she called the boy Ichabod, saying, "The glory has departed from Israel."

1 Samuel 4:21a

Ignominy is universally acknowledged to be a worse punishment than death.

—*Benjamin Rush*

The one thing that set ancient Israel apart from other nations was their connection with the Ark of the Covenant in which God's glory resided. The Almighty chose the descendants of Jacob (Israel) to be the "custodians" of His presence. Because of His nearness, handling the Ark was considered a sacred duty, and it was to be carried only by Jewish priests using two long poles fit through a set of rings.

The Ark itself was a wooden chest, overlaid with gold, and adorned with two angelic cherubim. Inside had been placed the two tablets of the Ten Commandments, a jar of manna, and a branch from an almond tree—reminders of God's dealings with the Israelites just after their exodus from slavery in Egypt (see Hebrews 9:1–5).

The Ark of the Covenant marked Israel's success. Through its power, Israel experienced financial prosperity and victory over its enemies. Unfortunately, people also began to view the sacred relic as a kind of "magic charm" to be used at will. Have you ever tried to use God for your own selfish purposes? Such attempts *never* end well.

During a dark time in Israel's history, the nation struggled under the oppression of the powerful Philistines. With the hopes of drawing upon the Ark's power, Israelite elders called upon Hophni and Phinehas, two wicked sons of Eli the high priest, to carry it into battle. Huge mistake! The all-wise King of Glory cannot be manipulated.

On that fateful day, Hophni and Phinehas were slain. To make matters worse, the Philistine army captured the Ark of the Covenant. Upon hearing the dreadful news, Eli fell from his chair and broke his neck. At about the same time, the wife of Phinehas uttered her last words while giving birth to a son. An expected day of supreme joy had turned to infamy because the nation's leaders had attempted to use God's presence rather than allowing Him to use them.

> And about the time of her death the women who stood by her said to her, "Do not be afraid, for you have given birth to a son." But she did not answer or pay attention. And she called the boy Ichabod, saying, "The glory has departed from Israel," because the ark of God was taken and because of her father-in-law and her husband. She said, "The glory has departed from Israel, for the ark of God was taken." 1 Samuel 4:20–22

The Hebrew word *ichabod* essentially means "no glory,"[1] or "inglorious," if you will. Forfeiting God's glory was the worst thing that could have happened to Israel. On that fateful day, the heart of national identity was ripped from Israel's chest, the shame of it all seemingly heaped upon the shoulders of a newborn child.

The sad tale of Ichabod's birth helps illustrate the grim reality of our human condition. The day that Adam and Eve pursued independence from their Creator was the day God's glory departed from humanity. From a spiritual perspective, every child is born an Ichabod, beset by an innate glory deficiency.

Few metaphors are perfect, but we can compare the idea of a glory deficiency to the disease of scurvy often suffered by ancient mariners. A simple lack of vitamin C led to chronic exhaustion, the loss of teeth, spontaneous bleeding and open sores, and even personality changes such as sadness and irritability. Similarly, because we were created in the Almighty's magnificent image, the human psyche cannot function properly when deficient in glory.

Can you imagine trying to treat scurvy with fake vitamin C tablets? No number of pills would alleviate the symptoms of the disease. Human glory is much like a fake vitamin, with the exception

---
1. James Strong, *Enhanced Strong's Lexicon* (Woodside Bible Fellowship, 1995).

that powerful moral ramifications are at play. Trying to fill a significance-void with vain human glory can never make us spiritually and emotionally healthy; we need the real thing. The unconditional love of family and friends can temper the devastating effects of lost glory, but woe to those who grow up in loveless environments. Their trauma at the hands of other humans only intensifies the dysfunction of a glory deficiency.

I have seen Christian leaders attempt to stamp out pride by constantly reminding people they are nothing more than terrible and undeserving sinners in desperate need of God's grace. And while such an idea is inherently true, fixating on our "ingloriousness" will not only create a breeding ground for anxiety and depression, it will also keep us enslaved to sin. Children who grow up in these environments seem to come away especially damaged.

Many of our struggles are "ichabod-induced," being the result of unfulfilled cravings for validation. Humanity's bane is that we seek to satisfy a deep-rooted glory deficiency with a cheap—although it does not come cheaply—substitute that does little more than counterfeit true and lasting significance. From the earliest age, we expend our energy in an endless quest for approval, only to realize its emptiness when life is spent and we approach death's door.

A primary problem with human glory is that it fades quickly, lacking the substance which marks the majesty of the divine. Even glory received from being in God's presence will fade if that nearness is not maintained. Indeed, this is what happened to Moses whose face shone brightly after spending time close to God (Exodus 34:29–35 and 2 Corinthians 3:7–18). *Only as we remain near to our Creator's presence will our lives be continuously bathed in His glory.*

A glory deficiency causes an insatiable thirst for validation. Think about your life for a moment. To what degree has the pursuit of significance influenced your thoughts, words, and actions? Have you felt the need to make a name for yourself? Have you exhausted body and soul in an effort to prove your worth? Have you sought to accumulate wealth, titles, and degrees in search of validation? Does the threat of public humiliation strike fear in your heart? Rare is the soul who sees through the facade of pseudo-glory, which keeps our species standing on the tips of its toes and reaching for the heavens.

Two deadly errors seem common to the human race: we either celebrate and proclaim our innate human glory, or we rivet our focus on the lack thereof. The former makes us feel better, but deceptively, because human glory is but an illusion. And the latter? Feeling miserable about ourselves does nothing to improve our situation.

Some spiritually minded people seek to break free from the prison of human approval by looking inward for a "divine spark"—that vestige of God's image that has been buried beneath worldly mindsets and pursuits. But there is no divine spark apart from a covenant relationship with God through the person of Jesus Christ. We are all Ichabods in search of fleeting validation, descendants of the devastated, with the trauma of Eden embedded in our DNA.

The Christian Bible firmly establishes our lack of glory apart from our Creator (Romans 3:10–18), but thankfully, the story does not end with our failure (Romans 6:23). In John's Gospel, we read that Jesus came to humanity "full of grace and truth" (John 1:14), and that "of His fullness we have all received, and grace upon grace" (John 1:16). These passages fill me with hope!

Our Lord's grace abounds like water in the ocean, and it comes to His children in wave after refreshing wave. Furthermore, God's amazing grace not only washes away our sins and gives us favor in His eyes, it also empowers us to become something greater than we could ever be on our own. He is the King of Glory who longs to restore our lost glory through a meaningful and endless connection to His presence!

QUESTIONS

1. Why is it a huge mistake to attempt to manipulate God?

2. What are some indications of a glory deficiency?

3. Why is it dangerous to continually focus on our unworthiness?

FURTHER READING: Exodus 34:29–35 and 1 Samuel 4

PRAYER: Lord, I confess my inclination to spend my life pursuing significance. Please lead me to glory that will never fade.

DAY NINE
NOTHING BUT POSSUM GLORY

Do not be afraid when a man becomes rich,
When the glory of his house is increased;
For when he dies he will carry nothing away;
His glory will not descend after him.
Though while he lives he congratulates himself—
And though men praise you when you do well for yourself—
He shall go to the generation of his fathers;
They will never see the light.
Man in his pomp, yet without understanding,
Is like the beasts that perish.

Psalm 49:16–20

A cannonball only travels six hundred leagues an hour; light travels seventy thousand leagues a second. Such is the superiority of Jesus Christ over Napoleon.

—Victor Hugo

Floating on water is one of my true pleasures in life. One summer afternoon, my wife Debi and I loaded our canoe on the roof of our SUV and headed for a reservoir we had never before visited. Our trip took us away from the main roads and along rolling fields through some of the prettiest farm country western Pennsylvania has to offer.

As we drove the forty minutes to the boat launch, I found myself pondering the names of small towns along the way. Several of them—and many others in our area—were the namesakes of "coal barons" whose companies extracted huge amounts of the mineral about a century ago. Colver, Revloc (Colver spelled backward), Adrian, Iselin, Luciusboro, and Waterman are all small western Pennsylvania communities whose names can be traced to wealthy coal company executives.

Another such town, Heilwood, was originally called "Possum Glory." The area once abounded with wild opossums (aka possums), so I suppose the name was given for obvious reasons. Ironically, adult possums are ugly, inglorious creatures. I should know; years ago, I had an unpleasant encounter with one in my garage.

The old coal mines of western Pennsylvania hold a prominent place in my family history. My grandmother immigrated from Hungary, and she lost two Hungarian husbands (although rumor has it that she never married my grandfather) in the mines. A third was injured so badly that he had to quit working.

Having listened to family stories, and having also worked for a large coal company, I am well aware of the hardships that my ancestors faced. They were not stupid people (my grandmother ran a store during the Great Depression while raising ten children, and her last husband spoke several languages fluently), but they were uneducated. A lack of schooling left them ripe for exploitation by shrewd businessmen with deep pockets and powerful connections.

The contrast between the coal barons and their immigrant employees could not have been more extreme. The former built extravagant mansions and employed personal servants to reach the fullest heights of luxury and comfort. The immigrants, who were brought to the United States for the sole purpose of working in the mines, often lived in company houses and made purchases from company stores. Unscrupulous business executives were known to fix the miner's expenses to be slightly more than their income. Worse still, working conditions in the mines were horrid and dangerous. My grandfather met his death in one such mine after being run over and mangled by a shuttle car.

I am not anti-business and recognize the opportunity that companies provide to people in the form of decently paying jobs. At the same time, when viable laws are absent or unenforced, unscrupulous business leaders will rise to dominate our corporate landscapes. These tycoons shrewdly wield power to build wealth at the expense of the masses.

In recent years, many corporate executives in the United States have selfishly schemed to skyrocket their own salaries while compelling employees to work longer hours with fewer benefits. The system is both sad and unjust, leaving those affected feeling powerless and disenfranchised.

Sadly, this type of economic oppression is nothing new. The powerful have exploited common laborers throughout human history. Biblical times were no different, and the Scriptures address this issue from a perspective that upends our natural mindsets:

> But the brother of humble circumstances is to glory in his high position; and the rich man is to glory in his humiliation, because like flowering grass he will pass away. For the sun rises with a scorching wind and withers the grass; and its flower falls off and the beauty of its appearance is destroyed; so too the rich man in the midst of his pursuits will fade away. James 1:9–11

Do we grasp what James was communicating? *From a human viewpoint, material wealth is glory. But from God's perspective, the humble Christian who struggles under the thumb of an oppressive master sits in a lofty position.* What our world calls "glory" is little more than "possum glory"—an ugly and ignoble substitute for the real thing.

If there is no God, a "survival of the fittest" mentality defines the scope of our reality. But if indeed a just Creator brought us into this world, the oppressed have great reason to hope, while oppressors should shake in terror at the thought of their final breaths. The selfish and unjust oppressor is little more than a flower whose beauty lasts for but a moment. Further still, the wise and righteous Judge will one day bring every act of injustice into account. Greedy hearts might seem to prosper for a season, but justice will prevail in the end.

Throughout the pages of the Bible, we find woven a heavy thread proclaiming the futility of a materialistic lifestyle. Ironically, it is often death that opens our eyes by separating true glory from that which is false. Neither ornate caskets nor massive headstones can transport glory from this world to the next.

We are deceived to believe that all whose lives are filled with material abundance are especially favored by God. Wealth, status, power, and lofty titles might sound grand and appealing, but when selfishly attained at the expense of others, they amount to nothing more than possum glory. After all, if glory can be purchased with perishable money, how long will that glory endure?

Our world's perspective is convoluted. We esteem things that mean little in the eyes of eternity and callously regard that which heaven honors. Therefore, *if we want to prosper emotionally and spiritually, the critical first step is to recognize the difference between that which is true glory and that which is not.*

The Lord champions those seemingly inglorious souls who are oppressed by this world's system. Life's secret is for Christians to recognize *now* their lofty status in the eyes of the King of Glory. Instead of forever remaining helpless and forlorn victims, we can accept God's grace to help us overcome. He is not the source of our affliction, but He will use it to produce within us "an eternal weight of glory far beyond all comparison" (2 Corinthians 4:17). Unjust hardship is not our end; it is our opportunity.

Are you envious of the rich, or bitter about your situation? If you are a covenant child of God, your heavenly Father will work every difficulty to your benefit. Better still, He will reward every faith-filled response to hate and injustice with an eternal glory beyond measure.

Next time you find yourself feeling envious of others, I encourage you to gaze at a picture of an adult possum (the babies can be somewhat cute) and remind yourself that wealth, status, and lofty-sounding titles are nothing more than possum glory. Just like coal that burns for only a short while, their value will soon turn to ash.

QUESTIONS

1. Please read James 1:9-11. How does James' perspective conflict with our natural mindsets?

2. What makes envy so damaging?

3. How do we go from being victims to becoming victors in Christ?

FURTHER READING: Psalm 37:1-22 and Psalm 73

PRAYER: Holy Spirit, please free me from envy and a small-minded emphasis on possum glory.

DAY TEN
THE PALE BLUE DOT

───────◗●◖───────

What is man that You take thought of him,
And the son of man that You care for him?

Psalm 8:4

Even those who write against fame wish for the fame of having written well, and those who read their works desire the fame of having read them.

—Blaise Pascal

In 1977, NASA launched the Voyager I robotic spacecraft. Almost thirteen years later, the spaceship had traveled about 3.7 billion miles (6 billion kilometers). At the request of astronomer Carl Sagan, NASA technicians commanded the ship's camera to turn around and snap a few dozen pictures of our solar system. One particular image stopped scientists in their tracks.

The composite photo is mostly black with a few vague bands of light caused by the effects of sunlight on the camera. Sitting in one of those light bands is a speck of blue about the size of a dust particle. That barely visible spot is a planet with a familiar name: Earth.

The photo, dubbed the "Pale Blue Dot," provides a powerful perspective of our insignificance in the grand scope of the universe. Sagan questioned how humanity could feel so self-important when the insignificance of our tiny planet speaks otherwise. His enlightened mind found our "imagined self-importance" to be a "delusion."[1]

Planet Earth, you see, is our natural frame of reference. We arrive on this terrestrial globe knowing nothing about galaxies and quasars and supernovas. It is natural then that our worldviews become shaped by the limited information found within our

---

1. Carl Sagan, *The Pale Blue Dot: A Vision of the Human Future in Space* (New York: Random House, 1994), 7.

immediate life experiences. We spend the bulk of our lives posturing for prominence because we think that is all that matters.

With uncommon perception, Carl Sagan recognized the vanity of fighting wars and spilling blood for the sake of fleeting glory. He understood humanity's constant quests for supremacy to be meaningless in the overall scheme of the universe. Sagan, however, lacked a perspective that changes everything: *each person is the handiwork of a grand Creator.* At His touch, the intrinsically meaningless explodes with significance. Humans matter because the King of the Universe created us *in His image.*

Years of observation and learning tell me that most of our human dysfunction—including that in the church—is connected to a search for significance. Those who repeatedly taste the sweetness of success soon begin to revel in their supposed superiority. Others, in their failed quest for glory, become hapless Ichabods. They dwell in dark, lonely dungeons where our existence is meaningless, human life is cheap, and a grim sense of hopelessness permeates thought.

That the residents of this Pale Blue Dot long for significance is self-evident; it flavors everything we do. But why are we this way? Three reasons stand out. First, having been created in God's image, we are wired for glory. Second, having succumbed to the ultimate temptation, we continuously lust for glory. Third, having been separated from the King of Glory, we are born glory deficient. This "triple glory combo" woven into the fabric of human nature is why our individual and collective cries for glory cannot be silenced.

Trying to suppress the desire for significance is futile. And continually proclaiming our unworthiness does not make us humble, only self-centered. Instead, we must understand that our worth is directly linked to a covenant relationship with our Creator. We find true freedom only as we abandon the vaporous quest for human glory and learn to rest in the love and grace of our glorious King.

When the Almighty gazes across the expanse of the universe, He looks through and beyond the untold billions of celestial bodies, riveting His attention on the seemingly insignificant humans who populate an obscure planet. Created to rule in the very image of the sovereign God, humans are far more prized than animals and honored even above heaven's angels. I would not be surprised if it was the heavenly announcement of God's plans for humanity that triggered Lucifer's ill-advised quest for glory.

> When I consider Your heavens, the work of Your fingers,
> The moon and the stars, which You have ordained;
> What is man that You take thought of him,
> And the son of man that You care for him?
> Yet You have made him a little lower than God,
> And You crown him with glory and majesty!
> You make him to rule over the works of Your hands;
> You have put all things under his feet,
> All sheep and oxen,
> And also the beasts of the field,
> The birds of the heavens and the fish of the sea,
> Whatever passes through the paths of the seas.
> O Lord, our Lord,
> How majestic is Your name in all the earth!
> Psalm 8:3–9

Is God not capable of mega-magnificence and micro-love at the same time? *We are each **somebody** in the grand scheme of our massive cosmos because the Maker of all things sees us as significant.* Truly substantive glory is found within the gleam of our Creator's eye.

The secular message of the cosmos tells us that we are nothing more than meaningless specks of organic matter soon to return to earthly soil. But the eternal message of the gospel proclaims that the King of Glory values us even above His own well-being. Human societies are filled with dysfunction and violence because the full message of the gospel has not taken root in our hearts.

Oppressing others for the sake of superiority indicates that we are clamoring to find significance in a world without meaning. Belittling and dehumanizing those who differ from us only serves to broadcast our own insecurities. And being caught up with positions and titles reveals that the truth of the gospel has not fully permeated our hearts and minds.

Establishing the contrast between human and divine glory is essential because the well from which we draw glory has a massive influence on virtually every aspect of life. The heavens declare the profound majesty of God, but all too often, the behavior of professing Christians proclaims His smallness—a mistaken tragedy of epic proportions. Our bickering, our divisions, and our smug sectarianism all serve to cast a dark pall upon a faith that is in every way glorious. Only as we become secure in our identities as God's royal children can we begin to deal effectively with the inner dysfunction that promulgates the human condition. If we do not learn to see ourselves through the eyes of our Creator, death will fester and have sway even as we live out our transitory existence on this planet.

Heaven continues to shout to humanity, "In My glorious image!" But when our ears are deaf to the heavenly trumpet, we are left to grasp for vain significance. Devoid of true glory, we then expend our life's energy in pursuit of junk-store substitutes. By the grace of the Almighty, we can do better.

Jesus Christ willingly stepped down from His glorious throne in heaven, endured extreme public humiliation, and then suffered a torturous death on this Pale Blue Dot so that He might bring us into His family and elevate us to lofty heights. Apart from Him, we are nothing. In Him, we are galactic kings and queens!

QUESTIONS

1. How is our human sense of significance affected by a distorted and inaccurate perspective of the God who lovingly created us?

2. What message about human value does the gospel communicate?

3. Why is it vital that we learn to see ourselves as God sees us?

FURTHER READING: Isaiah 53 and Romans 5:6–11

PRAYER: Heavenly Father, thank You that the secular message of the cosmos is a lie and that my life is beyond valuable because of Your incomprehensible love for me.

PHASE ONE REFLECTIONS

Deep within every human heart stirs a virtually unquenchable appetite for affirmation, approval, and adulation. This innate quest for glory is a universal human trait that has produced some of the most tragic injustices in history. (Day 1)

One of the secrets to life involves recognizing the difference between human glory, which always fades, and the glory of God, which endures *forever*. Unfortunately, we naturally focus our attention on fading glory. True, substantive glory has nothing to do with the passing opinions of others and everything to do with real and lasting significance. When we fully grasp the difference between mere image versus true substance, we are freed to live the glorious lives our Heavenly Father designed for us. (Day 2)

Humanity has known kings of all kinds, including the widely influential cultural king of rock 'n' roll, Elvis Presley. Jesus, however, is the *King of Glory*—the self-existing God who reigns over all with unimaginable power and ability. To pursue glory apart from Him is to enter into a world of dysfunction. (Day 3)

Through His life, death, and resurrection, Jesus revealed true glory. We can find enduring significance only through an ongoing connection with the majestic King of kings and Lord of lords. As we align ourselves with God's wise design, we can experience the power of heavenly glory in amazing ways. (Day 4)

Lucifer was thrown from heaven because he sought to overthrow God and steal His glory. Much to our detriment, the powers of darkness tempt us virtually nonstop to live independent from God and to find significance through self-effort. This is the ultimate temptation—to try to be like God apart from God—and it is within this self-sufficient quest that the power of sin takes root. Any journey toward liberty, victory, and hope for a meaningful future must include learning to triumph over the ultimate temptation that entices us to find significance through self-effort apart from our Creator. (Day 5)

When Adam and Eve disobeyed God by eating from the tree of the knowledge of good and evil, they were separated from His presence and found themselves naked and ashamed as a result. Shame, guilt, and condemnation are all comrades of misery that keep us mired in fear and subject to manipulation. Our hope for wholeness and freedom lies in Christ's power to banish the comrades of misery from our lives. (Day 6)

Feeling the toxic effects of shame, Adam and Eve used fragile fig leaves in an attempt to cover their nakedness. Those leaves are symbolic of the figurative leaves that we use to avoid ridicule by presenting a stellar outward image to others. Performance, appearance, possessions, status, knowledge, and associations with others are some of the metaphorical fig leaves humanity continues to use to mask its naked vulnerability. (Day 7)

Attempts to hide our shame never endure. Since humanity is no longer clothed in God's glory, we are all born with a glory deficiency that makes us feel like Ichabods who have no glory. This deficiency can never be fulfilled by human effort because no matter how hard we try to cover ourselves in an attempt to gain glory from the world, we will never be truly satisfied. Thankfully, Jesus Christ is the King of Glory who longs to restore our lost glory through a meaningful connection with His presence. (Day 8)

Far too many people mistakenly spend their lives pursuing wealth, status, and power. These constitute nothing more than possum glory—a deceptive substitute for the real thing. All kinds of injustices result from this blind pursuit, but we must understand that the oppressed who are in Christ are the ones to be envied. Whatever earthly glory people might obtain, it will always be temporary and pale in comparison to the real thing. (Day 9)

We are tempted to regard glory on this earth (that which is seen) higher than that of eternal glory (that which is unseen). A haunting photo from the Voyager I spacecraft reveals our planet to be nothing more than a speck in our solar system. In our immense cosmos, human life would be insignificant if not for the mysterious favor bestowed upon us by our Creator. Because of Jesus, the inhabitants of this Pale Blue Dot are elevated to an unimaginable status when they enter into a covenant relationship with the King of Glory. (Day 10)

PHASE TWO
SEEING WHY IDENTITY MATTERS

> Do you not know? Have you not heard?
> Has it not been declared to you from the beginning?
> Have you not understood from the foundations of the earth?
> It is He who sits above the circle of the earth,
> And its inhabitants are like grasshoppers,
> Who stretches out the heavens like a curtain
> And spreads them out like a tent to dwell in.
> He it is who reduces rulers to nothing,
> Who makes the judges of the earth meaningless.
> Scarcely have they been planted,
> Scarcely have they been sown,
> Scarcely has their stock taken root in the earth,
> But He merely blows on them, and they wither,
> And the storm carries them away like stubble.
> "To whom then will you liken Me
> That I would be his equal?" says the Holy One.
> Isaiah 40:21–25

Having established the contrast between fading and lasting glory, we will now explore the dysfunction caused by the pursuit of fading glory. Laying such a foundation can be an unpleasant, albeit necessary, endeavor. We cannot fully embrace God's good plans for us without first coming face-to-face with the error of our own ways. Furthermore, if we cannot accept the more difficult truths of the Bible, we will not believe those which seem too good to be true.

If you see yourself in this phase of our exploration, you are not alone. None of us are exempt from the identity struggles that are common to all humanity. Just keep moving forward, one step at a time, because after we face our challenges here, in Phase Three we will learn about some incredible and encouraging truths.

DAY ELEVEN
GLORY AS A DRUG

Behold, You desire truth in the innermost being,
And in the hidden part You will make me know wisdom.
Psalm 51:6

There is more hunger for love and appreciation in this world than for bread.
—Mother Teresa

Nicki's drug addiction contributed to having three children to three different men—none of whom she married. She then destroyed her daughter's kidneys by neglecting to get medical attention for a urinary tract infection. A kidney transplant failed because she did not give the little girl her anti-rejection medicine. Nicki loved her kids, but her addiction led her down dark, self-centered roads, and she ended up losing them. Her drug abuse also brought grief to her aging father as she stole his money and neglected his grandchildren. A final, lasting grief came from her untimely death due to an overdose.

Drug addiction has become a huge problem in more than one society during recent centuries. It takes only a distant connection to an addict to get a sense of the deep despair and pitiful circumstances that mark a substance-abuse existence. Being closely connected further reveals the sad reality of our human condition.

An addict's life can be characterized by the contrast between dazzling highs and devastating lows. Drugs create powerful feelings of euphoria, but they never last. Eventually, the high fades, only to be followed by a painful reality that renders the previous high a faint dream. The horrid physical and emotional feelings that accompany a downward crash leave an addict willing to do just about anything to restore lost euphoria. Lying, stealing, and prostituting one's body are all common in the imprisoned world of addiction.

One might think that addicts are people of only low degree—those who live in poverty-ridden circumstances and have little hope for a meaningful future. This is simply not true. Addiction knows no bounds; the wealthy can be as easily ensnared as the poor.

The glory of approval and success, in many ways, is also a drug that respects no boundaries. The fact that we are wired for glory, combined with our inherent glory deficiency and lust for glory, makes us all *glory addicts*.

A glory high is amazing! Few feelings of elation and euphoria can compare to human applause. But much to our dismay, no amount of praise or affirmation will ever satisfy our appetites for significance. When the glory fades, as it is known to do, the resulting "ichabod feelings" can quickly cascade into misery. As glory slips through our fingers, we often respond like a drowning victim—trying desperately to grab onto someone or something to keep us from going under. Our attention then fixates on past accomplishments or on connections with people we deem to be significant.

Just as drug addiction leads to personal, familial, and societal dysfunction, so does glory addiction. When our attention fixates on the pursuit of significance and validation, we might lie, cheat, destroy our bodies, or sleep with people we would otherwise find repulsive. What extreme sacrifices we make for glory!

The human psyche cannot function well without routine "injections" of glory. Thus, we all crave the significance of being a successful "winner" in life and despise the shame of losing. We drink freely of glory's high, then slink into unbearable despair when it is gone. Consequently, our addiction to glory becomes an inescapable trap from which only God can free us.

Unlike our Creator, our sense of glory is bound to our feelings. I once heard a star athlete responding to questions after winning a coveted championship trophy. "What is it that keeps you motivated to put in the long hours and hard work required to win a trophy?" a reporter queried. The star's reply? "The feeling that I have right now!" Temporary moments of powerful pleasure stir within us lasting cravings for more.

Reveling in the glory of human adulation creates a sense of pride—often leading to attitudes of arrogance and elitism. The opposite side of the spectrum—being devoid of human approval—brings its own painful array of dysfunctional issues. These struggles warrant exploration because they profoundly influence our lives regardless of whether we choose to acknowledge and understand them.

Not only must we be aware of the issues that define us, we also need wisdom to navigate through them. A legalist, for example, might say that because the pursuit of greatness makes us prone to assaulting heaven's throne, we should squash all human aspirations and forbid any involvement that speaks of competition. History teaches us, however, that the "suppression route" never works. Because humanity has been created in God's image, the desire for greatness is inherent. Thus, it should not be stymied, but rather managed wisely. The secret is to stay closely connected to God, to draw our sense of significance from our relationship with Him, and to channel our feelings of accomplishment back toward the One who created us.

Our demise lies not with the desire to do great things, but with worldly thinking that pursues greatness independent of God's glory. Such a self-sufficient approach creates an environment ripe for arrogant and elitist attitudes.

Before going into greater detail about wisely managing our pursuit of greatness, we must address some of the dysfunction that results from our never-ending pursuit of significance. Facing these realities can be a painful endeavor, but three basic steps will help establish a healthy pattern for breaking the bonds of a glory addiction:

> 1. **Be honest.** The first step to overcoming any addiction is to admit that we have a problem. Unfortunately, one of the symptoms of a glory addiction is an inability to admit weakness or wrongdoing. Most of us feel that we do not sin—we simply "make mistakes." Furthermore, because we are addicted to the need for significance, we can easily sink into a self-condemning turmoil when the reality of our true state begins to surface. Still, we must learn to be objectively honest with ourselves, even when it hurts. Neither elusiveness nor self-deception will do us any favors. Instead, we must turn our focus to God's good plan.

2. Pursue an understanding of how God sees you. The pain of feeling like an Ichabod can be extreme, but the Lord has something better for us. The solution to our glory addiction is to see ourselves as He sees us. Self-honesty is necessary because only honest eyes can perceive God's reality. We have no glory apart from an intimate connection with the King of Glory.

3. Give glory back to God. As the Lord lifts us from the ashheap of brokenness, our struggles with pride do not mystically disappear. When feeling good, we will be tempted to glide along the easy-flowing trade winds of self-glorification. The key to staying humble, though, lies not in making ourselves miserable or denying God's great work in and through us. Rather, turning all glory back to Him in the form of thankfulness, praise, and worship is how we produce the mysterious antidote for pride. Only through worship and thanksgiving can we revel in glory without our hearts being corrupted by its euphoria.

Whether we speak of drugs, alcohol, sex, or glory, all addictions are deeply rooted and painfully conflicting. But hope is never lost as long as we are willing to turn an expectant gaze to our Savior. He understands exactly how we are wired and will wisely guide the seeking soul to wholeness and freedom.

QUESTIONS

1. In what ways can glory be compared to a drug?

2. What are three factors that contribute to a glory addiction?

3. Which of the three basic steps to break free from a glory addiction challenges you the most?

FURTHER READING: Psalm 18:25–36 and John 12:36–43

PRAYER: Heavenly Father, You alone are able to meet my deepest needs for significance and free me from the need for human approval. Please lead me deeper into the truth that sets me free.

DAY TWELVE
STAIRWAYS TO HEAVEN?

For by grace you have been saved through faith; and that not of yourselves, it is the gift of God; not as a result of works, so that no one may boast.

Ephesians 2:8–9

I wouldn't trust the best fifteen minutes I ever lived to get me into heaven.

—Adrian Rogers

"When Justin [Martyr] was arrested for his faith, the Roman prefect demanded that he denounce his faith by sacrificing to the gods. Justin replied, 'No one who is rightly minded turns from true belief to false.'"[1] The prefect then had Justin beheaded for subverting the Roman Empire.

The Bible overflows with messages of love, inspiration, and hope, but it also causes conflict and creates a breeding ground for hatred toward those who adhere to its tenets. Why? Both the Old and New Testaments contain statements of exclusivity that cast other belief systems in a poor light.

In the Old Testament, frequent admonitions challenged the Jews to worship only one God (e.g., Deuteronomy 6:13-14), essentially proclaiming all other gods—and thus, all other religions—to be imposters. The majesty of those gods, according to the Bible, was nothing more than the skillful creation of human hands. Idols are little more than shallow images lacking true substance and ability.

> The idols of the nations are but silver and gold,
> The work of man's hands.
> They have mouths, but they do not speak;

---

1. "Justin Martyr: Defender of the 'true philosophy,'" *Christianity Today*, accessed April 02, 2024, http://www.christianitytoday.com/history/people/evangelistsandapologists/justin-martyr.html.

> They have eyes, but they do not see;
> They have ears, but they do not hear,
> Nor is there any breath at all in their mouths.
> Those who make them will be like them,
> Yes, everyone who trusts in them.
> Psalm 135:15–18

Despite what the psalmist penned, ancient Israel continually worshipped idols; the stern warnings of the prophets went largely unheeded. Archaeologists have confirmed this fact through the discovery of large numbers of idols in ancient Jewish homes. Only through a seventy-year exile in Babylon, which was directly attributed to their idolatrous worship, did the Israelites learn a painful lesson and begin to worship only the God of their ancestors. This purity of worship then created a set of new difficulties by offending other nations that honored their own beloved deities.

The Son of God did not make the situation less difficult when He walked this earth. On more than one occasion, Jesus proclaimed Himself to be God in human flesh (John 8:58–59; 14:6; and 20:26–29). Christ's followers then held His exclusive deity as a core doctrine, making them objects of scorn in the eyes of Roman officials who found such thoughts offensive to their sense of religious plurality.

Opponents of unwavering religious belief rightly claim that such "narrow-minded devotion" creates cultural conflict. Those critics who still consider religion to be vital to life often take their claims a step further. "All paths," they contend, "lead us to the same God." Such statements can be made with altruistic hearts, but they oppose the teachings of the Bible. Thus, we are left with three basic options regarding our approach to Christianity in light of other religions.

> **1. We accept the Bible as the inspired, infallible, and authoritative Word of God** (thus offending adherents to other belief systems). The Bible does not stand alone apart from God, but rather serves as a tangible expression of His wise authority.

> **2. We accept all religious texts as equal, relegating most conflicts to allegorical writing, scribal errors, or textual

changes made by over-zealous adherents (thus offending the God of the Bible).

3. **We reject all religious texts as human fabrication** (thus offending most everyone except atheists).

While I agree that all religions share a certain measure of common ground, several elements of Christianity set it apart from the rest. Understanding the history and nature of our human glory deficiency plays a vital role in helping us grasp why all religious paths do not lead to the same God.

A unique aspect of New Testament teaching involves the means by which people find favor with God. Every other belief system is "law-based." What I mean is that every other religion requires us, by self-effort, to attain to some standard, rule, practice, etc. Christianity alone frees us from this requirement in a way that does not lead to chaos.

Law-based religion creates a "stairway to heaven" approach to appeasing the divine. We are told that if we can be good enough, give enough, pray enough, and follow the necessary rules, we can climb a glorious staircase to the heavens. And while this approach might seem reasonable, it also presents massive problems.

Humanity ever glories in its own accomplishments, and the idea of climbing a stairway to gain God's favor is no different. During the course of our supposedly upward journey, there will be times when we stop, catch our breath, and reflect on our progress. It is then that our troubles intensify. When we believe we have succeeded, boastful thoughts of self-achievement flood our minds. Our world has seen no small number of pompous religionists confirm this tendency. Conversely, if we think our progress has stalled or crashed, we will feel guilty, condemned, and ashamed. All manner of sinful, dysfunctional, and self-destructive behaviors then result.

In climbing a stairway to heaven, it does not matter whether we think that we have succeeded or failed. Simply attempting to ascend to God's throne through self-effort feeds and fuels the power of sin (Romans 7:5 and 1 Corinthians 15:56–57). This is because human nature continues to proclaim, "I will ascend to the throne of glory!"

Moral self-accomplishment provides our old fallen natures with an opportunity to fulfill their glory quests apart from a relationship with God—even when we do so in His name.

How does Christianity differ from all other belief systems? *The Bible teaches us that the ability to rise to heaven is not something we possess; rather, it is a gift from God (Ephesians 2:8-9).* The stairway to heaven is more like an elevator which relies on a power beyond ourselves. Furthermore, since "all have sinned and fall short of the glory of God" (Romans 3:23), we can stop and enjoy the view to the top without our egos being inflated. No one is worthy of the ride, and all glory, we know, belongs to God. If not for His amazing grace, we would be stuck on the ground in our Ichabod ways.

Forging a path that only He could, Jesus bore the full brunt of the temptation toward self-glorification. Of all who have ever walked this earth in human flesh, the Son of Man alone has triumphed over the "I will ascend!" mentality. His victory has become our salvation! Christianity, in its essence, then, must be exclusive.

I hesitate to criticize those devoted to other belief systems. Still, I challenge everyone to thoroughly explore the issue of glory and its ramifications regarding religious practice. As the apostle Paul wrote two millennia ago, "Christ is the end of the law for righteousness to everyone who believes" (Romans 10:4), and "there is salvation in no one else; for there is no other name under heaven that has been given among men by which we must be saved" (Acts 4:12).

QUESTIONS

1. Why is the message of the gospel inherently offensive?

2. How is Christianity uniquely different from other belief systems?

3. What are some of the problems caused by taking a "stairway to heaven" approach to religious practice?

FURTHER READING: Acts 4:1–12 and Romans 10:1–13

PRAYER: Lord, I will never be able to hit the mark of Your majestic glory. Please forgive me for trying, and teach me to rest in Your grace.

DAY THIRTEEN
SIN AND SIGNIFICANCE

For am I now seeking the favor of men, or of God? Or am I striving to please men? If I were still trying to please men, I would not be a bond-servant of Christ.

Galatians 1:10

It is not the being seen of men that is wrong, but doing these things for the purpose of being seen of men. The problem with the hypocrite is his motivation. He does not want to be holy; he only wants to seem to be holy. He is more concerned with his reputation for righteousness than about actually becoming righteous. The approbation of men matters more to him than the approval of God.

—Augustine

The date was March 23, and the air was brisk with spots of snow dotting the landscape. In the early hours of the morning, while deep in thought, I ambled toward my college dorm. A friend had just turned my world upside down with a simple question: "What's holding you back?" I had been seriously contemplating becoming a Christian for several weeks but found myself hesitant to take such an all-inclusive step. Now, Karen's well-timed query was compelling me to honestly consider the reasons for my hesitance.

I did not need a college degree to realize that I was afraid of the cost of becoming a follower of Christ. More specifically, I feared losing my two closest friends. "Getting religion" would mean a new way of life—one out of step with our past patterns of thought and action. I do not think, however, that I grasped how much those friendships influenced my sense of identity. Nor did I comprehend that the source of my identity would be intricately tied to living out the Christian faith to which I was being called.

When Adam and Eve reached for the fruit of the tree of the knowledge of good and evil, they did so to be like God apart from God. Is this not an identity issue? That single act of disobedience unleashed an avalanche of destruction, suffering, and death, and it stemmed from a pursuit of glory independent from our Creator. The quest for glory, we must understand, is no trivial pursuit.

Why is it vital that we see the original sin in such a light? *If sin is rooted in an identity problem, the path to victory over sin must be an identity solution.* Furthermore, we are compelled to think of the gospel—the good news of Jesus Christ—as an *identity message*.

One of the more damaging mistakes Christians have made throughout the years involves presenting the message of the gospel and the message of identity as two separate concepts. The two, in fact, are inextricably connected, and it is to everyone's advantage that we present them as such. Our heavenly Father does not just concern Himself with where we are going, but also with who we become.

A key reason we have largely failed to connect salvation and identity is because of a critical oversight in our understanding of the apostle Paul's writings. In predominantly secular societies, such as many in the West, identity and religious observance are not closely related. But in a religious culture—such as the Jewish environment in which Paul lived—faithful religious observance helps to form the core of a person's identity.

> If anyone else has a mind to put confidence in the flesh, I far more: circumcised the eighth day, of the nation of Israel, of the tribe of Benjamin, a Hebrew of Hebrews; as to the Law, a Pharisee; as to zeal, a persecutor of the church; as to the righteousness which is in the Law, found blameless.
>
> But whatever things were gain to me, those things I have counted as loss for the sake of Christ. More than that, I count all things to be loss in view of the surpassing value of knowing Christ Jesus my Lord, for whom I have suffered the loss of all things, and count them but rubbish so that I may gain Christ, and may be found in Him, not having a righteousness of my own derived from the Law, but that which is through faith in

Christ, the righteousness which comes from God on the basis of faith. Philippians 3:4b–9

I cannot remember ever hearing verse seven—"those things I have counted as loss for the sake of Christ"—quoted in its original context, that of identity. Most often, this passage is used in a much broader sense, as in referring to our possessions, relationships, and dreams. While such an application no doubt applies, Paul was emphasizing his *religious* identity, which in Jewish culture reflected his *entire* identity.

This simple realization leads us to one that is even more profound: when Paul wrote about living under the law, he was speaking about both his acceptance in the eyes of God *and* his sense of significance in the eyes of his peers. Do we grasp what Paul was communicating? *The gospel is not only a message of future destiny, but also present identity.*

Imagine, if you will, walking down a corridor through multiple doors leading to a secret passage; one door leads to another. In a similar vein, seeing the gospel as an identity message opens our eyes to the fact that living in victory over the power of sin requires that we find a new path to significance in this world—one that runs contrary to the natural course of human thinking.

Virtually all cultures tie identity to how we look, what we do, what we own, and the people with whom we associate. In essence, we spend much of our lives laboring *for* validation. Taking things a step further, we also seek validation through our good works. Therefore, doing something significant makes us significant. But laboring to gain significance presents a huge problem because it sends us climbing those long, steep steps up the virtual stairway to heaven.

Biblically, our identity comes from our intimate connection to God, while our words and actions are the *results* of who we are. Serving God can be profoundly meaningful, however, and so we face a powerful temptation to esteem ourselves based on the value of our service. It might seem thin at times, but a line exists between *doing something significant for God* and *working to find significance for ourselves*. We triumph over sin only as we labor *from* significance and not *for* it.

The sinful nature that each of us has inherited from the human bloodline continually seeks to establish a sense of significance apart from our Creator. This means that the gospel is also a message of *repentance*. We are called to make a 180-degree turn away from self-driven lives and to direct our thoughts and actions toward Him instead. Subsequently, one of the key elements of repentance involves *how* we establish our sense of significance. Humans labor—almost without ceasing—to become "weighty" in their subcultures in order to be seen as significant. However, it is not our work which validates us, but rather our connection to God. *As Christians, we break from cultural norms by receiving our significance as a gift from God and then spending our lives serving others from that place of security.*

Understanding the relationship between sin and significance powerfully influences our ability to understand the New Testament, and Paul's writings in particular. *Faith establishes who we are, and love determines why we serve.* Once our eyes are opened to this ever-present reality, we will view Paul's teachings about living by law in a new and fresh light.

Positive change happens only as we reverse our natural course and labor with the full assurance that we are *already* accepted as the beloved and chosen children of God. This change, however, does not come naturally or easily. We cannot simply will ourselves to think differently. We must receive from our Creator a deep-rooted sense of validation that flows only from His glory.

QUESTIONS

1. Why must we learn to see the gospel as an identity message?

2. How does our quest for significance apart from God affect our ability to live in victory over sinful desires?

3. What does it mean to repent?

FURTHER READING: Genesis 3:1–19 and Romans 7:1–6

PRAYER: King Jesus, please open my eyes to the importance of finding my identity through a relationship with You.

DAY FOURTEEN
REJECTION HURTS

―――――――▶●◀―――――――

The stone which the builders rejected
Has become the chief corner stone.
This is the Lord's doing;
It is marvelous in our eyes.

Psalm 118:22–23

Remember, the pain of rejection is nothing compared to the pain of regret.

—Matthew Hussey

Whether we call it a formal, a ball, or a prom, many high schools throughout the world celebrate the ending of a school year with a formal dance. In the United States, "prom royalty"—a king, a queen, and their courts—are chosen by popular vote.

Peer pressure seems to peak during prom season, with attendees often spending far more money than they should to satisfy the thirst for social acceptance. When I was in high school, we faced considerable pressure to have a prom date; few people in that era went as singles.

For the most part, traditions ruled, and males did the asking, while females responded with an exuberating "yes" or a devastating "no." The experience was usually awkward, not to mention that it created an emotional roller coaster for those who felt that failing to secure a prom date was about the worst thing that could happen to an air-breathing human.

Feeling the pressure myself, I made my move early and landed a date with a nice girl who was a year younger. This early success meant that I could relax and watch the "who's taking who" intrigue play out for the next few weeks. Unfortunately, the prom-induced drama hit a bit closer to home than I had expected.

Year in and year out, school administrators organized our homerooms and their seating by alphabetical order. Spending fifteen to twenty minutes every weekday with the same classmates over a span of several years meant that we would inevitably build friendships. One homeroom friend (I'll call her Sally) was a genuinely nice girl who socialized with the popular, athletic crowd. Although part of the cheerleader squad, Sally did not fit the movie stereotype of a cheerleading snob enamored with her own persona. She was down-to-earth and friendly, and I often enjoyed joking around with her as we waited for the school day to begin.

Although we got along well, I never considered asking Sally to the prom. Believing that she was above my social sphere due to her cheerleader status,, I assumed someone else would ask her and save me the humiliation of being refused. But nobody did—ask her to the most important social event of the century, that is.

Sally was devastated. I can still picture her sitting at her desk crying inconsolably as a flood of tears streaked dark lines of mascara down her reddened cheeks. Here she was, a supposedly popular cheerleader, and no guy thought enough of her to extend an invitation to the senior prom. Sally was an awesome young woman, so popularity was not an issue. But in her mind (Does anyone really know what goes on in a teenager's mind?), she was an outcast, a reject, an Ichabod. Thankfully, Sally's senior prom was salvaged at the last minute by a merciful friend who had graduated the year before.

We fell out of touch after graduation, but the memory of Sally's unpleasant experience has stuck with me. Regardless of whether we have had a similar prom experience, we can all relate to the pain of rejection Sally felt. Rejection cuts like a knife, its razor-sharp edge piercing the depths of the human soul. Why does the pain run so deep? Being excluded sends an unwelcome message: you are insignificant, inglorious, and unloved. For a species wired for glory, but born with a glory deficiency, rejection scrapes the bottom of our emotional experiences.

Our responses vary when we are pushed outside the circle of acceptance. Some people cry. Others lash out in anger. Still others withdraw into their own isolated worlds. Almost all of us are naturally inclined to harden our hearts and erect walls of self-protection.

We have just cause to mask our vulnerabilities—and with a vast array of fig leaves mind you. As much as we might wish otherwise, this world can be terribly cruel. Selfish, petty, and untrustworthy people are never in short supply to torment, bully, criticize, and exploit those who show signs of vulnerability. I find it sad to admit, but self-aggrandizing agendas are the human way.

Rejection is especially painful when we care deeply about those who exclude us. And when we have developed relational intimacy, the pain of rejection is multiplied even more. Thus, we tend to emotionally distance ourselves by closing off the vulnerable places of our hearts so no one can hurt us again. Unfortunately for us, this approach is rooted in an unhealthy form of self-trust that not only alienates us from other people, but from God as well (see Jeremiah 17:5–8). Consequently, healing becomes elusive and our pain perpetual.

The fear of rejection constrains our lives and constricts our ability to experience the full vitality of life our loving Lord desires for us. Driven by the fear of shame and rejection, we fashion self-protective fig leaves to project an image of significance in line with current cultural standards.

All is not lost, however! As we proceed on this journey of finding significance in Him, we can take a couple more steps to break free from the vice-grip of human approval:

1. Thank God for the opportunity to identify with Jesus. Much can be said about identifying with Christ in this regard.

First, because He was betrayed by one of His own disciples (Judas), and because He was rejected—to the point of being unjustly crucified on a wooden cross—by the very people He came to help, Jesus understands the pain of rejection.

Second, the pain of rejection provides an opportunity for us to draw nearer to God, learn His ways, and conform to His image.

Third, Jesus' early followers considered it *an honor* to suffer mistreatment, rejection, and scorn for His sake (Acts 5:41). Being publicly shamed for God's honor is to our glory.

> Finally, God will not waste our difficulties. If we respond to rejection with love and faith, instead of bitterness and hatred, the Lord will use our situation to help others in amazing ways.
>
> **2. Find a trusted friend or counselor with whom to share your struggles.** Rejection can make us feel ignoble and worthless, often leading to a dangerous, self-imposed prison of isolation. Shame thrives in lonely, dark dungeons. Talking to a loving, trustworthy, and mature person about our struggles allows the love of God to touch our hearts through His human servants.

No one has been rejected the way Jesus has. Stepping down from the glory of heaven to lift up struggling humanity, the Son of God was rejected by His community, betrayed by a close associate, denied by a best friend, and sent by His own people to be crucified. It is safe to say that Jesus knew something about the pain of rejection, and yet He chose to keep moving forward in the midst of inconceivable hurt.

Being rejected can be intensely painful, but it does not need to be debilitating. The Lord intimately understands our struggles and welcomes us to identify with Him. He also seeks to place people around us who genuinely care. We, however, need to respond with faith, be open to His leading, and keep moving forward step-by-step.

QUESTIONS

1. Why does the pain of rejection run so deep?

2. How does being rejected give us an opportunity to identify with Jesus?

3. What are some of the blessings that God can bring out of the pain of being rejected?

FURTHER READING: John 15 and Ephesians 3:14–21

PRAYER: God, You are the Great Physician. I surrender my walls of self-protection and ask You to permeate and heal the broken and isolated places in my heart.

DAY FIFTEEN
CANCEROUS INSECURITY

> Then he [Saul] said, "I have sinned; but please honor me now before the elders of my people and before Israel, and go back with me, that I may worship the Lord your God."
>
> 1 Samuel 15:30

Insecurity's best cover is perfectionism. That's where it becomes an art form.

—Beth Moore

Despite his flagrant character deficiencies, David—Israel's second king—remains one of the most beloved personages in that nation's illustrious history. David was passionate and devoted to God, but also cocky and self-righteous at times. An affair—or was it rape?—with Bathsheba, followed by a devious plot to kill a faithful ally (Bathsheba's husband), led David to humble himself and cry out to God for mercy. The Lord heard the king's sincere plea, which is why both Jews and Christians continue to hold David in high regard.

The reign of the first Israelite king—Saul—is not characterized by fond memories, although he began well enough. Handsome in appearance while standing head and shoulders above the crowd, he seemed like the masculine stuff of which kings are made. Regrettably, Saul had a significant problem: he was insecure (1 Samuel 15:17).

Insecurity can be described as self-doubt or lack of confidence resulting from a glory deficiency. Insecurity causes us to be self-centered, continually looking for acceptance, approval, and affirmation. When insecure people are not approved or validated according to their expectations, they tend to either sulk or throw temper tantrums, spreading their misery like gangrene.

Saul made more than one significant misstep because he lacked a firm sense of identity. First, the king disobeyed God because he was afraid that his followers would disapprove of his actions and abandon him. He then lied to Samuel the prophet (a prophet is the last person to whom you want to lie). Later, when God began to bless the shepherd boy David as the king in waiting, Saul became intensely jealous and attempted to take David's life. The fear of his lineage losing the monarchy so consumed Saul that he blindly pursued a destructive course of action.

Due to our inherent glory deficiency, we are all susceptible, but with some, the problem of insecurity is especially pronounced. My own struggles go back as far as my earliest memories. My parents, who had separated not long after my birth, eventually got back together, but my dreams for happiness failed to materialize. They argued frequently, and neither was able to give me the attention and affirmation that my most important developmental years warranted. We lived in a low-income housing project, and my interaction with school classmates continually reminded me of that fact. I also lacked many of the qualities that made for school-age popularity, and so I found myself feeling like a nobody in a nowhere town.

Thankfully, despite my ignoble beginnings, God has done an amazing work in my life, and insecurity does not have the hold on me it once did. *As ingrained as insecurity might be, it is not a permanent personality trait, but rather the fruit of a life deficient in both love and significance.* I must remain vigilant, however, because during difficult times, I am often tempted to allow old insidious thought patterns to again pollute my mind and corrupt my words.

I now understand insecurity to be a deadly, deceptive beast that consumes us from the inside out, destroying our most valued relationships in the process. It is no stretch to compare it to a cancer eating away at all that is living and vibrant. Insecurity also leads to rationalized self-justification, which then breeds delusional thinking. Do you remember the story of Cain and Abel? Cain murdered his brother because God had a higher regard for Abel's sacrifice. Who does something like that? Cain's insecurity became sin's opportunity.

Because of past struggles, I know insecurity well and can often spot it readily. Sadly, its selfish presence "de-graces" Christian circles far more than we want to admit. I have seen insecure people wreak havoc on church worship teams, stealing the spotlight that should be on God by turning the focus back to themselves. I have seen Christian leaders deny devoted people the opportunity to serve with their God-given gifts because those abilities threatened to outshine the "ministry star." And I have seen pastors put up emotional barriers to protect their vulnerable selves, creating all kinds of ministry dysfunction because of their unwillingness to trust anyone.

Insecurity contaminates the purity of our motives and steals our focus from truly honoring the King of Glory. It also hinders the advance of His purposes as we endlessly stroke sensitive egos and negotiate soap-opera-like drama. Make no mistake about it, when unchecked and allowed to have sway, insecurity will impede the growth of even the best ministries.

Addressing insecurity can seem like trying to suture a gash on an angry tiger's paw. An insecure person will often view loving correction as a personal attack, making honest, rational discussion practically impossible. Personal honesty requires significant courage because an insecure individual cannot bear being seen as flawed.

Extremely insecure people leave those who care about them with one of two primary options. The first is to do everything possible to placate the touchy individual. We will feel as though we are living to appease, but conflict *might* be kept to a minimum. The other approach is to confront insecure behavior with a delicate combination of gentle and firm resolve. Depending on the person and the situation, the results will vary, but I think the best hope for meaningful change lies on this possibly rough road. My main hesitation would involve confronting those with violent tendencies.

An insecure heart is never satisfied—even when "fed" a steady diet of approval. Steps to confront such self-centeredness must be taken gently, prayerfully, and wisely. The core issue involves identity, but insecure individuals often seek to control all manner of people and circumstances.

In Christian organizations, especially, we dare not allow self-centeredness to steal the glory that belongs to God. Nor can we allow an insecure person to continually hamstring our efforts to reach the world with His love and truth. The well-being of the people we serve is more than worth the conflict and discomfort that addressing insecurity will bring.

Furthermore, we will never effectively advance God's purposes without constructive input from others. When I first began writing books, for example, receiving editing input felt like being stuck with pins. Due to my insecurities, the exposure of my writing imperfections made me feel less significant as a person. Now, I covet the input of a skilled editor, recognizing that my ability to influence others increases considerably with wise and insightful feedback.

Read through 1 Corinthians, and you will see that Paul devoted much of that letter to problems related to insecurity—although the word itself is never used—among Christians. Our Lord loves to call insecure people to Himself, but He hates allowing them to stay that way. God's glory is powerfully displayed when He takes people who are nobodies in the eyes of this world and forms them into selfless servants who live with a burning passion to bless others.

If you struggle with insecurity, you are not alone; I have seen figures as high as ninety-five percent. Please join me in giving the Lord the freedom to root it out of our lives. When situations arise—and they will arise—that bring our insecurities to the surface, let us confront them with painful honesty. Only then will we be able to see the fullest scope of God's purposes become reality in our lives.

QUESTIONS

1. How does insecurity hinder us from becoming all God wants us to be?

2. What problems can result when a Christian ministry allows insecurity to go unchecked?

3. What are some wise and loving steps we can take to address a person's self-centered insecurities?

FURTHER READING: Psalm 51:1–13 and 1 Corinthians 1

PRAYER: Dear God, please grant me the grace to face my own shortcomings, along with the wisdom to lovingly deal with others as they struggle to break free from self-centeredness.

DAY SIXTEEN
OPENED BUT CLOSED

And Jesus said, "For judgment I came into this world, so that those who do not see may see, and that those who see may become blind." Those of the Pharisees who were with Him heard these things and said to Him, "We are not blind too, are we?" Jesus said to them, "If you were blind, you would have no sin; but since you say, 'We see,' your sin remains."

John 9:39–41

In the country of the blind, the one-eyed man is king.
—*Desiderius Erasmus*

One of my favorite Bible stories is that of Jesus healing the man born blind (John 9). What drama followed! Befuddled by this obvious miracle, the Pharisees sought to discredit the man's story but could find no grounds for doing so. Finally, frustrated that these religious leaders were pressing the issue to the point of ridiculousness, the man with restored sight confidently stated that Jesus must have been sent from God. The Pharisees threw him out of the synagogue.

For his atrocious "sin" of being healed by Jesus, synagogue leaders excommunicated the man born blind from the social and religious community that had defined his existence from his earliest days. Still in a huff, some Pharisees listened intently as Jesus found the rejected man and encouraged him by affirming His deity.

Through the tense conversation that followed, the Pharisees acted as though they could see spiritual matters with impeccable clarity, but it was confidence in their *own* ability to see that kept them blind to God's ways. They are by no means alone in this sense.

The Pharisees' response bears similarities to what transpired in the garden of Eden. After eating of the forbidden fruit, Adam and Eve's eyes were opened (meaning they became aware of good and evil) while simultaneously becoming closed (meaning that they became blind to their Creator's ways). I sometimes contemplate the irony that while being opened, their eyes were also closed. What was it, I am inclined to wonder, that darkened their sight? And why have we each been born spiritually blind since then, unable to see and understand God's ways?

We find a hint of the answer in Jesus' proclamation, "As I hear, I judge; and My judgment is just, because I do not seek My own will, but the will of Him who sent Me" (John 5:30). Jesus was implying that self-serving motives skew our perception. The Son of Man could see *everything* clearly because His heart was entirely pure and free of self-serving motives. Not so with the rest of us.

The group of Pharisees that Jesus chastised in John 9 could not see because they could not—or would not—admit they were spiritually blind. Just as Adam and Eve scurried to find fig leaves to cover themselves, so too, the Pharisees feverishly labored to keep their naked souls from being exposed.

Admitting their ignorance would have turned the Pharisees' world upside down for several reasons. First, their self-aggrandizing self-images risked being shattered. Second, as God's supposed representatives and teachers of Israel, they feared losing the confidence of the people by presenting a less-than-perfect image—a struggle still common among leaders. Third, the Pharisees refused to admit they were spiritually dull-sighted because it would have threatened their prestige, power, and wealth. Although they claimed to serve God, these influential men displayed a history of serving their own interests over His.

Of all the motives that influence our actions, few possess the influence of the universal drive for *self-preservation*. Insecure souls who are bound by the compulsion to feel significant *must* see themselves in a positive light. They demand that others do so as well. Anything less is offensive and unacceptable. A lifestyle of defensiveness and self-deception results as they find themselves unable to entertain perspectives that threaten their hyper-sensitive psyches.

The following negative tendencies often characterize those driven by a quest for self-preservation:

- They find it painfully difficult, if not impossible, to admit when they are wrong.
- They loathe revealing personal weaknesses.
- They make self-justification a way of life. Their actions might not make rational sense to others, but they have a reason for everything that they do. Personal deception then reigns, as their own minds become adept at deflecting any input that might cause them to feel bad about themselves.

We are all born with closed eyes. Whether they remain closed is largely dependent upon our willingness to move beyond a limited existence defined by self-preservation. As with the man born blind, those who wish to see must be willing to take risks. At times, we must risk the disapproval of our loved ones. Circumstances might also warrant risking rejection from our peer communities. And perhaps most challenging of all, we must be willing to risk the emotional consequences of admitting our inability to see.

I find it ironic that we so often work frantically to avoid appearances of vulnerability because we are afraid of the cruel judgments of others. Our stubborn refusal to receive loving correction then sets the stage for worse judgments. No doubt, this world is replete with cruel souls who relish an opportunity to make us miserable, but there are also genuine and caring people who want the very best for us.

None of the steps toward breaking free from a self-preserving mindset are meant to be taken independently. When God calls us to travel a difficult road, He promises to stay with us through thick and thin. After all, it was Jesus who sought out the man born blind after he was rejected by the Jewish leaders. Our loving Savior recognized the blind man's need that resulted from His own healing touch, and He refused to abandon him to the consequences.

Furthermore, isolating ourselves from other believers is never a good idea. All people—including leaders—must work through struggles and face personal shortcomings; it is our universal reality. By connecting with non-judgmental people, with whom we can share our struggles, we can avoid becoming hypocrites who broadcast fake images because of the fear of being judged.

Through flesh and blood humans, we can experience God's love in practical ways, which makes abandoning the church a bad idea. Of course, the kind of church we connect with will have a huge influence on our ability to let down our masks and images of perfection.

When we consider local church involvement, we must think about *health* and not *perfection*. Anytime we connect with people, we will face disappointments and let-downs; they are a part of our human reality. Even so, healthy churches exist where loving people face and work through their struggles together.

Churches that emphasize rituals over relationships and rules over love require perfect people as participants. And since perfect people are nowhere to be found, perfect images become necessary. It is no wonder that grace-deficient environments are rife with dysfunction. Where grace is lacking, the preservation of an image becomes tantamount. And when image matters more than anything else, our eyes are closed to an accurate perception of God's reality.

We each play a substantial role in our ability to see spiritually. By identifying and confronting our self-serving motives, we can humble our pride and position ourselves for God to heal our spiritual blindness. We can also look for—and work to create—grace-rich environments that allow others to do the same.

QUESTIONS

1. What factors might have prevented the Jewish religious leaders from admitting they were wrong (John 9)?

2. Why are leaders prone to present images of perfection?

3. How can we create a grace-rich environment that allows people to be honest with themselves and with others?

FURTHER READING: Matthew 23:13–27 and John 9

PRAYER: Oh, Lord, please forgive my image-induced blindness and open my eyes that I might see clearly.

DAY SEVENTEEN
MY KINGDOM OVER YOURS

Do not be afraid, little flock, for your Father has chosen gladly to give you the kingdom.

Luke 12:32

The kingdom belongs to people who aren't trying to look good or impress anybody, even themselves. They are not plotting how they can call attention to themselves, worrying about how their actions will be interpreted or wondering if they will get gold stars for their behavior.

—Brennan Manning

It all begins innocently enough. A gifted and motivated Christian leader sets out to do great things for God and the betterment of humanity—or so he tells himself. Working tirelessly to promote a compelling vision, he stirs hearts and gathers a devoted team to forward the mission of the organization.

Before long, their hard work begins to pay off. A church grows and increases its sphere of influence. A sports program wins games and launches into the playoffs. A business makes money and expands quickly. Regardless of the type of organization, God's blessings seem evident.

Too often, though, something is amiss; despite the outward success, an insidious process unfolds beneath the surface of the organization. The glory that belongs to the Lord is being subtly owned by the leader and his team. Each new step forward, each new win, each positive review contributes to a growing sense of ego-driven euphoria.

The outward message of the organization might sound fine: "We are but lowly servants of the King of Glory. He deserves all the praise." But inwardly, a sense of elitism grows. Self-praising thoughts such as, "Based on our track record of success, we are obviously a cut above the rest," begin to overshadow feigned expressions of humility.

Motives mean everything, so as an organization such as this grows, it builds a kingdom, but that kingdom is not God's. Instead, the popular leader becomes the monarch. Hidden motives determine destiny, and building such a feudal kingdom under the guise of laboring for God is far more common than most leaders care to admit.

Once these self-serving kingdoms are firmly established, they must be preserved. Human nature demands it. Power intoxicates, and so sharp, prideful talons squeeze authority tightly in order to maintain control. Equally sharp eyes guard that power—along with image and reputation—keenly watching for oncoming threats.

Essential to building and preserving a man-made kingdom is the painstaking effort to craft a favorable image. "Sincere," "devoted," and "sold out to the cause" are just a few of the labels that rising monarchs plaster upon themselves—in full view of their faithful subjects. Despite hidden, self-serving motives, their display of devotion and dynamic gifts inspire awe in the hearts of their followers. To the unsuspecting observer, it seems as though these superstar leaders are blessed above others because of a specially favored status in heaven's eyes.

When organizational prosperity combines with performance-based mindsets, the resulting pride creates a growing sense of entitlement. A toxic mix of selfish desires, interwoven with an entitlement mentality, cannot help but subvert the organization's integrity. Extravagant housing, pricey dinners (with cocktails, of course), and clandestine romantic liaisons can become self-justified perks of even faith-based organizations. Welcome to the world of celebrity living!

No matter whether an organization be sacred or secular, when it reaches the point where image matters most—regardless of the public image portrayed—it stands in flagrant opposition to God's good plans and purposes. The "my kingdom over yours" mentality is a primary reason we see so many scandals in the public sphere. It is why religious organizations cover up sexual molestation. It is why collegiate sports programs flaunt rules intended to protect young players. It is also why high-level government officials employ shrewd teams of public relations consultants and expend large sums of hush money to bury their indiscretions.

From time to time, a voice of integrity will attempt to bring correction, but it is attacked like a political rival in a hotly contested race. Because integrity threatens the image, and thus, the man-made kingdom, swift retribution seeks to silence that voice. Those who refuse to "toe the party line" are generally removed, ostracized, and discredited as disgruntled souls with self-serving motives. The irony of it all!

It does not matter if the motives of misguided leaders were cancerous from the beginning or if the decay set in at a later date. When image becomes paramount, protecting it becomes the top priority—especially in a culture quick to shame and criticize any perceived social deviance. If a stellar image cannot be maintained, the flow of funds into organizational coffers will slow to a trickle, and that is seen as the worst possible thing that can happen.

In spiritually minded settings, those called to be shepherds become wolves who are driven by an "I will ascend" motivation. Referred to in the Bible as *false prophets*, they feed off God's flock in pursuit of wealth, power, and elevated egos. No matter how charismatic, gifted, or educated such leaders appear, their path will lead followers away from truth and into a quagmire of deception.

Why is it vital to address these types of issues? Innocent and vulnerable souls will unjustly suffer if we do not. How do I know? I have watched far too many heart-wrenching scenarios unfold. I have seen reports of innocent children marred by sexual abuse. I have seen faithful people deeply wounded as they pursued what they thought was full-scale devotion to God's purposes. And I have seen grand "works of God" come crashing to the ground in a cloud of noxious dust. Some of those involved became hardened and alienated. Others disavowed future church involvement. Still others walked away from their Creator altogether, cynically reasoning that the God of the Bible is either nonexistent or full of lies.

Disheartening scenarios of organizational decay are painfully common, but they are also avoidable. A vital key to prevent the slide down this slippery slope lies in purifying our motives from the start.

It is never enough to pursue a vision for the glory of God and the good of humanity; we must also, from the very beginning, establish and protect the humble integrity of that vision.

In no way do I discount the importance of theological training, but how I wish that *identity training* were a part of every Christian leader's preparation for public service. Addressing the importance of godly character is not enough; we must also incorporate an understanding of the relationship between identity and character in our teachings. If only our organizations took more care to address these issues with prospective leaders *before* feudal kingdoms were erected and unblemished images fabricated! How much grief and heartache could be avoided? How much damage could be spared? How many souls could be saved?

There remains but one holy and unshakable kingdom that will stand the test of time. All others will crumble. Some will crash sooner. Some later. But make no mistake about it; every realm apart from God's will falter and fall. May we have the wisdom and devotion to move beyond giving lip service to our Lord's kingdom and establish an intentional approach that keeps us aligned with His eternal design.

If every Christian—and especially those in leadership roles—would honestly and thoughtfully address the dynamics of our natural human quest for glory, our world would be a far better place. As long as we have breath in our lungs, it is never too late to start.

QUESTIONS

1. What are some of the dangers of success?

2. What happens when a personal or corporate image begins to outweigh the importance of integrity?

3. What steps can we take to protect ourselves from the potentially corrupting influences of success?

FURTHER READING: Matthew 23:1–12 and Luke 20:45–47

PRAYER: Sovereign God, I surrender to You my kingdom that I might become a full citizen of Yours.

DAY EIGHTEEN
THE SOCIAL RIGHTEOUSNESS TRAP

So if the Son makes you free, you will be free indeed.
John 8:36

And, after all, what is a fashion? From the artistic point of view, it is usually a form of ugliness so intolerable that we have to alter it every six months.
—Oscar Wilde

Not long ago, I read about a twenty-five-year-old man who fell one hundred feet to his death while taking a selfie at the Long Men waterfall in China. When workers recovered the body, they found a picture of him in the process of falling to his death. That unfortunate fellow got a dramatic selfie but at the expense of his life.[1]

Selfie deaths occur when people (usually under thirty years old) put themselves in risky positions to get dramatic self-images that will generate approval (likes) on social media. People have died falling off buildings, being hit by trains, drowning in raging waters, and being mauled by wild animals in an effort to snap that one glorious self-portrait. Why would so many of our kind risk their lives for a picture? Because of a phenomenon I call "social righteousness." The term is not commonly used, but its influence is everywhere.

In a broad sense, I define righteous as "being viewed with right-standing because we meet expected standards." From a Biblical perspective, we are declared to have right-standing in God's—the highest possible authority—eyes when we live up to His perfect standards of love and morality. "Kingdom righteousness" is the term I use in this regard.

Knowing that it is impossible for us to attain moral perfection, our wise and loving Creator has graciously provided the opportunity

---

[1]. Zachary Crockett, "The Tragic Data Behind Selfie Fatalities," Priceonomics.com, January 29, 2016, accessed April 02, 2024, https://priceonomics.com/the-tragic-data-behind-selfie-fatalities/.

to be "clothed" in Christ's righteousness through His sacrificial death and resurrection. When we, by faith, enter into a covenant relationship with God through Jesus Christ, we are declared to be accepted and approved (i.e., righteous) in heaven's eyes. In a very real sense, Jesus graciously drapes His spiritual robe of perfection over our imperfect shoulders.

For its part, pursuing social righteousness involves seeking the acceptance and approval of other humans. In early societies, the primary social spheres were family and community; their opinions mattered most. With the advent of public schools, the opinions of classmates rose to prominence. Thus, being socially righteous might mean wearing a ridiculously priced piece of name-brand clothing because that is what the most popular kids at school wear. Adding to our challenges, technological advancements of the twenty-first century have created a whole new dynamic of social interaction in which elevating and shaming reign supreme. Due to social media, a "social authority" in my life might now be an entirely fabricated persona supposedly living on the other side of the globe.

In today's world, social media and high-risk selfies provide an opportunity for the ordinary, "invisible" person to be "somebody." The more "likes" an individual accumulates, the more validated he or she feels. According to Ohio State University researcher Jesse Fox:

> It's all about me. It's putting me in the frame. I'm getting attention and when I post that to social media, I'm getting the confirmation that I need from other people that I'm awesome.[2]

Aside from the risk of death by selfie, pursuing social righteousness through human approval has several massive flaws:

1. Social media "authorities" are chosen impulsively. The path to becoming a social authority is not clearly defined, and there are no formal elections. Instead, "lawgivers" are those who garner the most popularity, have the most money, or exert the widest sphere of influence. As a result, standards tend to be fickle.

---

2. Zachary Crockett, "The Tragic Data Behind Selfie Fatalities," Priceonomics.com, January 29, 2016, accessed April 02, 2024, https://priceonomics.com/the-tragic-data-behind-selfie-fatalities/.

2. Opinions change, and everyone has a different one. Would you like a few laughs? Do a web search for "worst fashion trends." Past glory meets today's jeers. But who says that today's fashion authorities are right? Skilled marketing executives manipulate public opinion to keep us enamored with the new and discontent with the old, but in the end, fashion is nothing more than somebody's opinion.

Opinion involves more than fashion, of course. In a religious environment, being "good" will get you applause and approval. But if a drug gang rules your sphere, being bad is seen as good, and those who are the "baddest" become the "best."

With billions of humans roaming this planet, there are almost as many opinions as people. Whose favor, then, do we court? *If the desire for human approval is what drives us, we can be sure that it will drive us into the ground.*

3. Seeking the approval of people puts us at odds with God. Claiming to have moved beyond the "guilt culture" used by religious authorities to control people, today's movers and shakers use public shaming as a means to do the same. But the old has become the new; "shame societies" have existed for centuries. Now, just as in the past, the fear of shame compels people to bow to the human will rather than the divine.

> In true shame-oriented cultures, every person has a place and a duty in the society. One maintains self-respect, not by choosing what is good rather than what is evil, but by choosing what is expected of one.[3]

4. What we call "freedom" is merely a different form of bondage. Cultural "progressives" have worked hard to discard traditional Judeo-Christian standards in lieu of a "new morality," but the new freedom is not as free as we are led to believe.

Modern generations might declare themselves to be liberated from old-fashioned morals, but they are not free from social

---

3. Paul G. Hiebert, *Anthropological Insights for Missionaries* (Grand Rapids: Baker Book House, 1985), 212.

standards—as is evidenced by the precipitous rise of "socially prescribed perfectionism" that is wrecking today's youth.[4] In short, those who rebel against conventional mores simply exchange one set of standards for another.

5. Social shaming binds us in a prison of fear. The pursuit of glory demands that we meet standards, and the fear of shame keeps us bound to social expectations. But if we live for human approval, we give others authority over our lives without due cause. While unable to meet the demands of their expectations, we will forfeit our own destinies by trying. How often do we fail to stand for truth because we fear criticism? How many God-ordained opportunities do we forgo because we are afraid that someone will disapprove? More often than not, the limits of our accomplishments are established by how much criticism we are willing to endure.

The glory promised by human approval is little more than the alluring trap of social righteousness. If it is freedom that we seek, we must find it in Jesus Christ.

QUESTIONS

1. How are kingdom righteousness and social righteousness similar?

2. How is public shaming via social media used to control people?

3. In what areas of life do we allow criticism to keep us from doing what is good, right, and needed?

FURTHER READING: John 5:39–44 and John 12:27–43

PRAYER: Jesus, I want to know true freedom. Please show me the way!

---

4. Thomas Curran and Andrew P. Hill, "Perfectionism Is Increasing, and That's Not Good News," *Harvard Business Review*, January 26, 2018, accessed April 02, 2024, https://hbr.org/2018/01/perfectionism-is-increasing-and-thats-not-good-news.

DAY NINETEEN
ROOTS OF CONFLICT

But God has so composed the body, giving more abundant honor to that member which lacked, so that there may be no division in the body, but that the members may have the same care for one another.

1 Corinthians 12:24b–25

The emotion of shame is the primary or ultimate cause of all violence, whether toward others or toward the self.
—James Gilligan, M.D.

The Bible starts happily enough, but by only the fourth chapter of Genesis, something is seriously amiss. Cain savagely murders his innocent brother. Two aspects of this first murder are especially telling. To begin, Cain was the first child born to the human race; in essence, he represents us all. Second, Cain killed his brother because of *jealousy*. Abel had been honored by God for his sacrifice, while the Lord's response to Cain's offering was anything but enthusiastic.

Please note that God did not initially reject Cain. He simply disrespected the older brother's offering (for reasons that continue to be debated). Even when Cain got angry, the Lord merely sought to correct his behavior, but that is not how Cain perceived the situation. For God to have regard for Abel's offering but not his own, was in Cain's eyes, to utterly disrespect his person. Bam! Abel was dead, and violence soon overtook the harmony of earth. By the time Noah was born, the race that had been created in idyllic peace was overrun with violence (Genesis 6:11).

How much violence has been perpetrated throughout history because of our glory deficiencies? Century after century, as villains have illegally murdered their hapless victims, armies have "legally" waged war in a quest for supremacy.

The root of violence begins with the cry of Lucifer's pride-filled heart and its resulting imprint on the fabric of human nature: "I will ascend!" When seven billion people simultaneously attempt to ascend to God's throne of supremacy, conflicts are inevitable. What a sharp contrast to our Creator's original design!

After Adam and Eve ate from the forbidden tree, fear and shame—emotions they passed to subsequent generations—were their first reactions. The fear of shame is why a warrior would rather fall on his sword than be captured by an enemy. Or why a father would have his daughter stoned for losing her virginity—through no fault of her own—at the hands of a rapist. Or why a man would choose to murder a person in cold blood rather than suffer the "devastating fate" of public humiliation. To this day, fear and shame continue to drive humanity into chaos and dysfunction.

During my elementary school years, we had a little saying we used in a weak attempt to save face: "Sticks and stones may break my bones, but words will never hurt me." It was a lie. Words can inflict deep pain, and the real message is, "Sticks and stones may break my bones, but shame will make me hurt someone." That someone might be the perpetrator of my offense, a romantic partner, a child, or maybe even myself.

Psychiatrist and author Dr. James Gilligan spent over twenty-five years working with violent criminals. In his groundbreaking book, *Violence: Reflections of a National Epidemic*, Gilligan, the former president of The International Association for Forensic Psychotherapy, makes the following statements:

> These personality traits are, in my experience, the main motives for violence: the fear of shame and ridicule, and the overbearing need to prevent others from laughing at oneself by making them weep instead.[1]

> People are incomparably more alarmed by a threat to the psyche or the soul or the self than they are by a threat to the body.[2]

---

1. James Gilligan, M.D., *Violence: Reflections on a National Epidemic* (New York: Vintage Books, 1996), 77.
2. Ibid., 96.

Feelings of humiliation produce unhealthy fears, compel us to blame others for our shortcomings, and lead to "self-medication," often resulting in addiction. Furthermore, *feelings and fear of shame give root to violent behavior.* Not all who are shamed turn violent, but those lacking a healthy sense of significance are especially susceptible.

I sometimes wonder how many mass shootings begin with some type of humiliation. The pain of shame can be so intense that it drowns out a person's perception of all that is good. Furthermore, violence is not only physical. Hatred toward those who shame us is a form of emotional violence that has the potential to turn both verbal and physical.

The idea seems counterintuitive, but Gilligan also asserts that *civilization* is a primary cause of violence.[3] He does not seem to have a problem with civilization itself, but with the *stratification* of civilized societies that results from basing human value on cultural standards.

If we think about it, just about every area of society is stratified in one way or another. And what are some of the "vital concerns" that might cause us to look upon other people with contempt?

- Placing a utensil on the "wrong" side of a dinner plate
- The unfashionable tint of a piece of clothing
- The color of a person's skin

Greatness, in our natural minds, comes from living up to the standards that have been established by our social authorities. Even Jesus' disciples vied for this sort of supremacy and bickered among themselves as a result (Matthew 20:20-28).

Conflict often begins with what I call "disproportionate glory." When we fail to recognize how much God values us, we grasp for significance by seeking to meet cultural standards. Some people do better than others, and inevitably, one group exercises its power to deem another group inglorious. The resulting disproportionate glory then generates feelings of contempt and hatred. The social structure soon stratifies, and disrespect becomes an unpardonable sin.

---

3. James Gilligan, M.D., *Violence: Reflections on a National Epidemic*, 235.

What is God's proposed solution to the problems of conflict and violence? The King of Glory gives a generous dose of honor to those who lack significance so no one is put to shame (1 Corinthians 12:22–25). When all people are viewed with the same measure of significance, animosity vaporizes like foggy mist on a breezy morning.

Nothing fills our emotional coffers with a sense of significance the way God's glory does. And when our emotional storehouses are full, peace settles into our land. Disrespect has no power to offend, and therefore, no violent outcome if there is no glory-deficient nerve for that disrespect to touch. *To be glory rich is to be unified; to be glory deficient is to be divided.*

As appealing as the concept of equal glory might seem, those who consider themselves to be the "genetically superior" will take offense to the idea. In their minds, they tower above others. But do not be deceived by this false, fleeting sense of glory! When we look down with contempt upon the less gifted, we forfeit an eternal glory that could otherwise be ours.

The gospel of grace is brilliantly designed. The Lord raises every Christian to the heights of glory, but due to our track record of sinful and selfish behavior, none of us can claim to deserve such favored status. Through God's plan for shared and equal glory, He has wisely laid the foundation for everlasting peace.

QUESTIONS

1. How can shame, or the fear of shame, lead to violence?

2. What is the problem with the stratification of glory?

3. Please read John 17:22–24. What was Jesus communicating about glory and unity?

FURTHER READING: Genesis 4:1–8 and Luke 22:24–30

PRAYER: Heavenly Father, may I know firsthand Your glory and be at peace with myself and others.

DAY TWENTY
FREE FROM THE GLORY QUEST

For we are not bold to class or compare ourselves with some of those who commend themselves; but when they measure themselves by themselves and compare themselves with themselves, they are without understanding.

2 Corinthians 10:12

Glory is fleeting but obscurity is forever.
—*Napoleon Bonaparte*

Have you ever played "the comparison game"? We all know how it works because we play virtually nonstop. Imagine, for example, that you walk into a room full of "important" people. What goes through your mind? "How am I dressed? How do I look? What should I say? What will they think of me?" In an instant, you realize you are underdressed. Even your best outfit falls woefully short *compared to* sharp tuxedos, designer dresses, and diamond jewelry—and those are the key words exactly: *compared to*. Comparison is the foundation of judgmentalism.

From a New Testament perspective, not all personal judgments are bad (John 7:24). Only when we judge to assign worth to people do the real problems begin. *We can—and should—make a clear distinction between making righteous judgments and living with a judgmental heart.*

When we compare ourselves to others, we usually assign value on a scale of social standards. If you see yourself as more successful than me, for example, you will rank yourself higher, which in turn makes you a "weightier" (i.e., more significant) person.

Comparison-based living not only generates conflict, it also drowns out our God-given identities. Each of us has been uniquely crafted by our Creator, and it is a huge mistake to measure ourselves by other people. Seeking to live up to man-made standards, we sacrifice the unique stamp of the divine upon our lives. I am not suggesting that we spurn all human standards, but that we seek to find the source of our significance elsewhere. This process begins, as has already been shown, with going back to our human roots.

Glory is as dangerous as it is magnificent. And so our Creator needed a plan that would enable humans to be crowned with honor without their souls being corrupted. That plan begins with the very things that often cause us to doubt His goodness: the tree of the knowledge of good and evil, combined with the lingering presence of the fallen Lucifer on our terrestrial globe. *The opportunity to eat from the tree of the knowledge of good and evil not only established the groundwork for freedom that love requires, it also provided a way to prepare human hearts to enjoy glory's euphoria without being corrupted by pride.*

By allowing all humanity to be imprisoned in sin (Galatians 3:22), the Lord set in motion an amazing coup d'état. Jesus then entered into our human brokenness, defeated the power of self-exalting sin, and provided the opportunity to receive a new spiritual heart. As out of control as the iniquity of this world might seem, it helps create an environment in which God can share His glory with a race of unworthy people. *Only those aware of—but not focused on—their propensity to do evil can be lifted high without becoming enamored by a meteoric rise in status.*

We have already seen that human glory is tenuous at best, and a deadly illusion at worst. History is replete with men and women who rose to renown because of great beauty, ability, or wealth. Today, most are not even remembered apart from a few meager historical records. Furthermore, even the most renowned historical figures, if they lived independently from the one true God, will be counted as Ichabods when heaven's roll call finally sounds.

If we are to continue on a path to freedom and significance—the two go hand in hand—we must firmly draw the line between human and divine glory. The glory of harvesting a bumper crop from farm or garden, for example, has little to do with us and everything to do with our Creator. It is God who makes everything grow; all we do is capitalize upon His majestic work.

Human glory is fickle and subject to forces beyond our control. Whether a person rises as a champion or sinks as a loser can depend on nothing more than where a ball happens to hit on a line or the imperfect judgment of a weary referee. Furthermore, the higher we climb on the ladder of independent human glory, the more of our souls we leave wallowing in the dirt. The brilliant lights of fame might shine above our names, but they can do nothing to satisfy the dark emptiness that emerges when the applause fades, and our surroundings grow silent.

The problem for humanity—and it is a massive one—is that we cannot simply will ourselves to stop craving significance. A glory deficiency must be satisfied. *If we want a truly substantive existence, we cannot help but seek the true and lasting sense of validation that flows from God's glory alone.* Only as we lay hold of the new can we fully release the old.

To illustrate, a person who struggles with chronic pain is easily prone to self-centeredness, because the pain keeps drawing attention back to itself. Only when that pain is healed, is the attention-grabbing voice finally silenced. Similarly, only as our innate glory deficiencies are satisfied are we free to take our eyes off of ourselves. But oh, how we fight against the healing process!

A friend's daughter once fell on a gravel road and scraped her knee. That wound needed to be cleaned for proper healing to take place, but little Sarah would have none of it. Why? The poor child howled with agony because the fresh wound hurt when touched. Emotional hurts can work the same way. We need loving but honest assessment of our pain, yet that is often the last thing we can accept. Instead, we offend easily, cast blame quickly, and rationalize continually. Healing—as precipitated by truth—can hurt, but nothing gets better without honesty.

Personal revelation provides an added component on the path to healing and freedom. From a Biblical perspective, a revelation is a disclosure. In this personal sense, I am referring to a deep-seated disclosure of who God is, how He sees us, and who He makes us to be. It is insufficient to simply remember facts about God's love. *We need a deep-rooted work of the Holy Spirit that meets our pressing compulsion to be validated.*

The Spirit's work in our hearts is often incremental, or step-by-step. Through a series of ongoing revelations, our needs are met and our compulsion toward self-centeredness is gradually broken. As we increasingly discover our identities, not through comparison but through revelation, the stage is set for the greatest freedom of all: the ability to "lose" ourselves for His glory. Comparison, then, becomes a non-issue with regard to identity because it ceases to matter.

Much of the remainder this book focuses on how we lay hold of a new identity in Christ. Moving forward, however, requires us to willingly surrender our glory quest to God, to move on from our self-preserving mindsets, and to count our flesh-based identities as loss for the sake of knowing Christ (Philippians 3:7-8). Embracing what God says through the Bible about His children is also vital to our success. If we fail to unite the Word of God with faith in our hearts, personalizing His truth will prove impossible.

The perfect and glorious Creator of all things has long wanted to free sin-bound humanity by clothing us anew with His glory. Even more, He seeks to manifest that glory in and through us. When personal revelation from God—which always aligns with the truth of His Word—becomes integral to our existence, He will transform both our individual lives and our relationships into reflections of His glory.

QUESTIONS

1. How does comparison-based living form the foundation for judgmental thinking?

2. When does judging others become unhealthy?

3. How does being imprisoned under sin (Galatians 3:22) enable us to receive God's glory without being corrupted by pride?

FURTHER READING: Romans 14:1–13 and Galatians 3:19–29

PRAYER: Dear God, please open my eyes and give me a deep-seated revelation of who I am in Your sight.

PHASE TWO REFLECTIONS

The human psyche cannot function properly without a healthy sense of significance. As a result, the glory we obtain from approval and success acts like a drug that respects no boundaries. Three simple steps can help us break free from our glory addictions: getting honest, learning to see ourselves through our Creator's eyes, and developing the habit of giving glory back to Him. (Day 11)

Many of us want to believe that all religions lead to a meaningful relationship with God, but the New Testament approach to human significance differs from the rest. One of the major problems with focusing on religious rules is that it creates a "stairway to heaven" approach to appeasing God. And while this approach might seem reasonable, it can actually contribute to our human dysfunction by *increasing* our propensity to sin. (Day 12)

Ever since Adam and Eve ate from the tree of the knowledge of good and evil with a desire to be like God apart from God, human sinfulness has been innately connected to an identity quest. Because of this, we *must* begin to see the gospel as an identity message. Our good works should be the overflow of having a secure identity, rather than serving as a means to establish our sense of significance. This difference is vital because we triumph over sin only as we labor *from* significance and not for it. (Day 13)

None of us are exempt from being rejected by others. Rejection almost always hurts, but it is especially painful when we lack a secure identity. We are all tempted to put up walls of self-protection, but if we trust God and seek His purposes through times of rejection, we will see Him do amazing things in and through us. Our heavenly Father will always use the hardships we experience to accomplish good things. (Day 14)

If we do not learn how to deal with our glory deficiencies God's way, we will likely find ourselves insecure and in continual search of human approval. Insecurity makes us self-centered and susceptible to both individual and group dysfunction. However, even though insecurity can devastate our lives and relationships, the Lord loves to save insecure people and make them confident in Him. (Day 15)

Unfortunately, our innate drive for self-preservation hinders us from honestly dealing with our personal shortcomings. If we refuse to face them, however, we blind ourselves to God's ways. Therefore, it is vital that we involve ourselves in grace-rich communities where people are free to drop their masks, work through their struggles, and lift one another to new heights in Christ. (Day 16)

Christian leaders who do not secure their identities in Christ are prone to building their own kingdoms in God's name. When this is done at the organizational level, it creates an entitlement mentality and gives more value to outward images than to people. Every Christian—and especially every leader—needs to understand the importance of identity because it is integral to our long-term spiritual health as we influence others. (Day 17)

Humanity's innate glory deficiency compels us to seek a form of "social righteousness" which makes us slaves to fickle societal standards. If we allow, the pressure to conform will put us under the thumb of human opinion while also alienating us from intimacy with God. If it is true freedom that we seek, we must find it in the person of Jesus Christ. (Day 18)

The pursuit of social righteousness leads to *stratification* within society. This creates animosity as some people and groups are elevated above others. It is here that the roots of conflict and violence are formed. We can obtain true and lasting peace only by embracing God's good plan to give more honor to those who lack. (Day 19)

Finally, as chaotic as human sinfulness might be, our individual and collective moral failures help us realize how unworthy we are of receiving God's glory. Nonetheless, He chooses to bestow His glory on us anyway! This revelation, combined with knowing the Lord's unconditional love, enables us to be lifted up by Him without becoming self-enamored. The Creator of the Universe *longs* to manifest His glory in and through His much-loved children, and this will surely happen as we learn to align our lives with His wise design. (Day 20)

PHASE THREE
FINDING REAL SIGNIFICANCE

> You made all the delicate, inner parts of my body
> and knit me together in my mother's womb.
> Thank you for making me so wonderfully complex!
> Your workmanship is marvelous—how well I know it.
> You watched me as I was being formed in utter seclusion,
> as I was woven together in the dark of the womb.
> You saw me before I was born.
> Every day of my life was recorded in your book.
> Every moment was laid out
> before a single day had passed.
> How precious are your thoughts about me, O God.
> They cannot be numbered!
> I can't even count them;
> they outnumber the grains of sand!
> And when I wake up,
> you are still with me!
> Psalm 139:13–18 (NLT)

God is pure, holy, and magnificent beyond imagination, while we are sinful, selfish, and beset by dysfunction. It is on these grounds that we approach our awesome Creator. Jesus lowered Himself to enter the human race, serving as the perfect mediator through whom we might become highly favored children of God. It is on this foundation that we both relate to and serve our heavenly Father. We must never forget the cauldron of sin from where we came, but we cannot focus on our unworthiness if we want to be spiritually and emotionally healthy. When we direct our attention more toward our shortcomings instead of whom He makes us to be, we are likely to become miserable, self-centered, and disobedient toward the great purposes for which eternity calls us.

DAY TWENTY-ONE
IN HIS IMAGE

Then God said, "Let Us make man in Our image, according to Our likeness; and let them rule over the fish of the sea and over the birds of the sky and over the cattle and over all the earth, and over every creeping thing that creeps on the earth."
Genesis 1:26

If our identity is in our work, rather than Christ, success will go to our heads, and failure will go to our hearts.
—Timothy Keller

Popular science tells us it happened about 3.5 billion years ago. The location was most likely an underwater thermal vent, or perhaps a pool of water sitting on the tumultuous surface of our still-young planet. I refer, of course, to the origin of life—an event that continues to intrigue and baffle even the most brilliant scientific minds.

Metaphysical naturalists tell us that the earth's "primordial soup mix" came to be without divine influence. An electrically charged spark then birthed primitive life into a pool of raw chemicals, and that life systematically organized and reproduced itself with astounding complexity. Through an excruciatingly long process of random mutations, feelings, thoughts, and moral capabilities developed and organized into the astoundingly complex, but otherwise ordinary, creatures we call "humans."

For reasons still unclear, humans also "evolved" to need a deep-rooted sense of significance. Though we are deemed to be nothing more than living blobs of organic matter in a vast cosmos of meaninglessness, our species has never been content to live without feelings of value, worth, and purpose.

The absence of a Christian worldview leaves us susceptible to naturalism's "survival of the fittest" mentality; those who bring the greatest perceived benefits to society are valued above others. Professional athletes, for example, earn more money than first responders because they "share" their glory with their fans.

The most prominent glory-related characteristics define both identity and existence. Family standing, appearance, race, intellect, athleticism, productivity, wealth, romantic relationships, moral track record—all are used as building blocks for a positive sense of identity. Conversely, physical flaws, weaknesses, addictions, disabilities, a lack of connections, and poverty are often seen as markers of those who offer little or no value to society. Whether we inherited the elements listed above, chose them, or had them thrust upon us, they naturally tend to become the focus of our thoughts, and thus, come to define who we are. The world around us continually reinforces this tendency to assign value based on social standards.

Another line of thinking tells us that we were created by one or more deities, but that our value is still performance-based. Consider the concept of reincarnation for example. Ideas about reincarnation flavor several cultures, but especially Hindu India where one's present state is considered to be the result of past decisions. Those on the high end of the caste system are believed to be there because they earned it by their actions in a past life, which is also true for the lowly. This mindset offers minimal opportunities for those already deemed "socially worthless." With a largely meaningless existence, they can only hope to do enough good to elicit a few words of praise, or to climb a step higher in a future life.

The Bible turns performance-based mindsets such as these upside down. Elements such as body shape, wealth, and social standing do not define us. Instead, our value and significance flow from what the sovereign King of the Universe says about us. He has woven our significance into the fabric of our being, and no amount of intellectual-sounding scientific theorizing can explain it away.

At the grand touch of the Almighty, living blobs of organic matter—that appear to be intrinsically meaningless—become focal points of heavenly attention. Humans matter because the King of Glory created us *in His image*. When we begin to understand who God is and what He thinks about us, we are set free from hopeless mindsets, and the core of our existence is transformed.

In His image—the Christian Scriptures make that statement about no other creature in our universe. Biblical accounts describe angels as profoundly glorious, yet the Scriptures say nothing about them being made in God's image.

> When I consider Your heavens, the work of Your fingers,
> The moon and the stars, which You have ordained;
> What is man that You take thought of him,
> And the son of man that You care for him?
> Yet You have made him a little lower than God,
> And You crown him with glory and majesty!
> Psalm 8:3–5

"A little lower than God." What that statement means for the afterlife, we can only imagine. What it means for our current existence, we are stretched to comprehend.

King David (author of Psalm 8) proclaimed both God's glory and humankind's significance. He had been a shepherd from his youth, having spent countless hours gazing at the majestic night sky. David extolled the glory of the heavens, but the reality of the cosmos is far greater than he could have ever dreamed. Our far-superior understanding of the universe only increases our sense of wonder toward our Creator, as well as His choice to fashion us in His image.

What does it mean to be created in God's image? We cannot say with exact certainty, but we can ascertain a few vital ideas:

- Humans have been given the freedom and capacity to love
- Humans are marked by a profound ability to reason
- Humans are born with a deep-rooted sense of justice
- Humans have been given authority over animals

The above list is by no means exhaustive, but it is significant. God created us in His likeness as representations of Himself. Each of us is a magnificent work of art, lovingly painted on the canvas of human flesh. Therefore, knowing our place in the grand scheme of the cosmos is essential to our overall well-being. We are not even close to being equal with the Almighty—there is only one sovereign King of Glory whose nature is perfect in every way—but God has chosen to honor us by creating us in His likeness.

Being created in God's image also means that every human, regardless of age, is wired for glory. Significance and greatness are innate desires because we have been designed in the likeness of the greatest of all living beings. None of us are truly content with the mundane; we all need elements of excitement, wonder, and glory to feel fully satisfied. Young children, for example, do not play dress-up as bums—they dream of being superheroes, stars, and princesses.

True vitality involves more than being entertained, more than watching other people live their dreams and riding on the coattails of their success. True life also goes beyond climbing the ladder of social significance. Through faith in Jesus Christ, we discover personal value and worth apart from our appearance, genetic make-up, or ability to perform. This revelation of our true worth then enables us to rise above the commonality and corruption of self-centered living to reflect God's majesty in unimaginable ways.

The difference between being a randomly evolved blob of organic matter and a purposefully created representation of God's image is massive. *We are significant because He has destined us to be profound expressions of His glory and majesty.* We could not have been given a higher honor, and for that He deserves praise!

QUESTIONS

1. What are some of the moral and emotional consequences of believing that we naturally evolved without divine influence?

2. What are the negative effects of valuing people based on what they have to offer, as opposed to them being created in God's image?

3. What do you think it means to be created in God's image?

FURTHER READING: Genesis 1 and Psalm 8

PRAYER: Lord, help me to embrace the truth that my value is based fully in You, and not merely on what I can offer society.

DAY TWENTY-TWO
IN OUR IMAGE

Then Jesus was led up by the Spirit into the wilderness to be tempted by the devil.

Matthew 4:1

His [Christ's] willingness was motivated not by what He saw in us but by what is inside of Him.

–Paul David Tripp

No figure in history compares to Jesus Christ. Great men and women throughout the centuries have displayed undaunted courage and accomplished amazing feats. Jesus, however, revealed a different sort of greatness—one that is essentially alien to the human race.

Jesus was a revolutionary, but He never bore a weapon. Jesus lived without sin, and yet sinners wanted to be with Him. Jesus loved the unlovable and touched the untouchable. His healing hands brought hope and freedom to a people crushed by the heavy thumb of oppression. Jesus fulfilled all the requirements of Old Testament law, but His actions outraged the religious establishment nonetheless.

Jesus was God *incarnate*—i.e., in human flesh. A mystery beyond human comprehension, He was both fully God and fully man. Most Christians tend to think of Him as "the Son of God," and rightly so, but Jesus most often referred to Himself by the Messianic title "the Son of Man" (Daniel 7:13-14). Why would the glorious Son of God willingly embrace such an identity? Because, as the "second Adam" (1 Corinthians 15:45-47), He was also the pioneer of humanity who taught us how to truly live.

The Lord was not content to create us in His image and then abandon us when we misused and abused our freedom. Instead, Jesus became a man, conforming Himself to *our* image. Why? He sought to redeem and restore human character so it might again reflect God's glory. Furthermore, because Jesus walked in our shoes, living an example of the life we are meant to follow, He intimately understands the reality of our struggles.

One of Christ's purposes on earth was to provide a model and standard for humility unlike anything this world had ever seen. Stepping down from the glorious heights of heaven, Jesus went from being the focus of angelic worship to unimaginable—and unjust—scorn, ridicule, and torture by sinful humanity.

Embracing the limitations of the human body, Jesus began His ministry years with two significant events. The first was His water baptism in the Jordan River; the second was a forty-day period of fasting in the wilderness. That second experience culminated with three temptations I see as integral to our topic of glory:

> "If You are the Son of God, command that these stones become bread." Matthew 4:3

> "If You are the Son of God, throw Yourself down; for it is written…" Matthew 4:6a

> "All these things [the kingdoms of earth and their glory] I will give You, if You fall down and worship me." Matthew 4:9

With each temptation, the devil tried to do with Jesus what he has done with every other human: draw Him into the "glory game." Imagine the dark lord saying with a sarcastic sneer, "*If* you are the Son of God, then prove it!" When that first attempt failed miserably, "old slewfoot" followed with, "*If* you are the Son of God, prove that Your Daddy loves You." Finally, the enemy of all goodness let his true intentions be known by presenting Jesus with an opportunity to revel in the power and glory of this world without experiencing the pain and shame of the cross.

Although Jesus had done nothing significant to this point of His earthly life, He also had no glory deficiency. And so, for the first time in human history, not a single enticement found its mark. During this time of weakness, Jesus must have held tightly to the words spoken by the heavenly Father at His water baptism: "This is My beloved

Son, in whom I am well-pleased" (Matthew 3:17). *Jesus, the Son of Man, did not waver in His identity because He chose to believe the heavenly Father's pronouncement over His life rather than succumbing to the devil's glory-based enticements.*

What began with the wilderness temptations, continued with Christ's turmoil in the garden of Gethsemane, and culminated with His public torture and crucifixion. The Romans used the cross as an instrument of shame to keep their subjects in line. Cruel executioners crucified criminal "lowlifes" naked and in public locations where others could see and hurl abuse. Furthermore, death by crucifixion took hours, prolonging the humiliation. A naked, bloody body dangling from a rough wooden cross proclaimed that anyone who dared to defy the Roman Empire was cursed and unworthy of even a decent death.

To make matters worse, Jesus was crucified outside Jerusalem's walls, near a city gate, where large crowds coming to celebrate the Passover could gawk at His disgraced figure being wracked by the throes of death. In the eyes of both Roman and Jewish onlookers, Jesus went to the grave a cursed man, suffering the most humiliating fate possible (Deuteronomy 21:23 and Galatians 3:13).

The Son of Man was so devoid of pride that He willingly descended to the lowest strata of human shame to identify with and redeem the people He loved. The Son of God could not have experienced a worse form of humiliation than to surrender control of Himself to crucifixion—spread naked with arms and legs nailed to wooden beams. Never before had God displayed such glorious virtue to the human race. On that fateful day, majestic love flowed from Christ's veins as He hung on the cross and forgave those who had so unjustly condemned Him (Luke 23:34).

Do you realize the power and significance that Jesus gave up for your benefit? What leader willingly surrenders his power and his glory? Jesus descended from the highest of heights to the lowest of depths for the sake of you and me. *The glorious Son of God conformed to our image and identified with the depths of our shame because He wanted to give us the opportunity to identify with the heights of His glory.* No greater measure of selfless love has ever been displayed on the face of this ego-driven planet.

Being crucified was one of the most shameful things that could happen to a person in New Testament times, but shame only has power over those who are glory deficient. Not just once, but at least three times—in the wilderness, in the garden of Gethsemane, and on the cross of Calvary—Jesus despised shame and overcame the ultimate temptation to seek glory within Himself apart from the heavenly Father.

We must not underestimate the significance of Jesus' decision to conform Himself to our image as the Son of Man. We are called not only to receive the benefits of His sacrificial life, but also to follow in His footsteps and emulate His attitude. How do we accomplish such a daunting feat? We must grasp and engrave upon our hearts the reality of who the heavenly Father proclaims us to be. Those who find significance and security in the Father's love have nothing to prove to the world around them.

We will each, at one time or another, be deemed glory deficient. Either God will expose our glory deficiencies to bring us to repentance, or the world will deride us for falling short of its fickle standards. Our response, which influences virtually every aspect of our being, centers on whose voice defines our existence. *Always, always, always, knowing and believing what God says about us is what matters most!*

QUESTIONS

1. Why did Jesus refer to Himself as "the Son of Man"?

2. Read Matthew 4:1–11. How were the devil's three temptations related to Christ's identity?

3. In what ways did Jesus display divine glory through His crucifixion?

FURTHER READING: Matthew 3:13–4:11 and Luke 23:33–49

PRAYER: Lord Jesus, thank You for going from the highest of highs to the lowest of lows that You might identify with us. Help me to know deep in my heart the identity that You proclaim over my life.

DAY TWENTY-THREE
THE FATHER HEART OF GOD

―――――▶◐◀―――――

"For God so loved the world, that He gave His only begotten Son, that whoever believes in Him shall not perish, but have eternal life. For God did not send the Son into the world to judge the world, but that the world might be saved through Him."

John 3:16–17

God is the archetypal Father; all other fatherhood is a more or less imperfect copy of his perfect fatherhood.

—F.F. Bruce

In the early years of television, *Leave It to Beaver* was a popular program in the United States. The show depicted an idealized version of mid-20th century, middle-class life. Its theme centered around the adventures of Theodore (Beaver) and his older brother Wally. For the most part, their dad (Ward Cleaver) was portrayed as a loving and wise father who helped his kids navigate life through their foolish and shortsighted decisions.

Now, many decades since *Leave It to Beaver* stopped being aired, the themes reflected in Western television and movies present a far different story. Fathers today are often depicted as absentee deadbeat dads, pompous jerks, or bumbling idiots who rely upon their children to keep them from foolishly taking the family to the brink of ruin. Is this change merely a reflection of a changing society, or have these programs contributed to our social ills? These issues are subject to debate, but I believe the media trend has helped foster a significant lack of respect among young people toward their parents, and toward older adults in general.

The true essence of fatherhood differs radically from the images so often painted by modern media. No one is perfect, but still there are fathers who love nobly, provide faithfully, and discipline wisely. Not only do these men teach their children how to "do life," they also provide security and a sense of significance—at least until the little ones become teenagers!

Proverbs 17:6 tells us that, "the glory of sons is their fathers." Certainly, mothers play a vital role in nurturing and raising their children, but fathers add their own unique contribution to the parenting process. In many ways, it is through their relationship with Dad that children develop the confidence they need to face this chaotic world. Not long ago, I attended an outdoor concert and saw a man relaxing on the grass with his two young sons leaning against him. They were content. They were at peace. They were secure.

This illustration reflects a greater spiritual truth: a deep-rooted sense of identity is found not in and of ourselves, but through an intimate relationship with our heavenly Father. *Just as children thrive best when they feel secure in their parents' love, all of humanity needs to feel secure in the arms of our heavenly Father.*

Unfortunately, just as the nuclear family has been severely undermined by cultural changes, our perspective of God as our heavenly Father has also been badly tainted. This "development" does far more damage than many of us realize. How we view God profoundly influences whether we believe what He says about us. We cannot rest confidently in the Father's love if we do not trust Him.

Our challenge is to see God for who He is, rather than through the darkened vision of a sin-infested world. We cannot physically climb into our heavenly Father's arms, but we can find contentment, peace, and security through a spiritual connection with Him. This process begins with coming to know the *father heart* of our Creator.

Thankfully for us, we cannot influence the fixed reality of God's character. He is who He is regardless of what any human thinks, says, or does. The apostle John made some significant statements in this regard:

> Beloved, let us love one another, for love is from God; and everyone who loves is born of God and knows God. The one who does not love does not know God, for God is love. 1 John 4:7–8

God is love. There are no conditions in which the Lord is unloving. He may seem to discipline us severely at times, but our Creator loves each of us equally no matter what we do. Some of us might feel unlovable, but our feelings have *zero* influence on the reality of His character, for God is love.

A child who grows up in an environment devoid of love and affirmation will often spend a lifetime trying to prove his or her significance. The fear of being deemed "inglorious" will then corrupt decisions both large and small. In contrast, being loved unconditionally provides a powerful platform from which we can deal with our personal shortcomings. *We do not need to be perfect to be at peace with ourselves—we need only to be loved.*

Intimately knowing and experiencing the heavenly Father's unconditional love is an essential key to personal growth. When we realize that He loves us regardless of our worthiness—or lack thereof—we are free to let down our guard. Such liberty gives us courage to face our shortcomings and weaknesses, and thus grow in both virtue and ability.

Our Father's attitude toward us is beyond profound. *Since God is love, and His love is perfect, He loves each of us with the same love that He has toward Jesus (John 17:23).* We are no less loved by our heavenly Father than Jesus Himself. Such a thought seems almost too good to be true, but that is only because of our distorted perspectives.

God's love for us is not simply a theoretical concept. He has demonstrated it to be true to the fullest measure by sending Jesus to die a sacrificial death on the cross to redeem us from our sins. The prophet Isaiah even described Christ's painful death on the cross as "pleasing" to God:

> But the Lord was pleased
> To crush Him [Jesus], putting Him to grief;
> If He would render Himself as a guilt offering,
> He will see His offspring,
> He will prolong His days,
> And the good pleasure of the Lord will prosper in His hand.
> As a result of the anguish of His soul,
> He will see it and be satisfied;

> By His knowledge the Righteous One,
> My Servant, will justify the many,
> As He will bear their iniquities.
> Isaiah 53:10–11

The heavenly Father was pleased to crush Jesus on the cross? How can this be? Is God sadistic? Does He enjoy seeing others squirm in pain? Not at all. Jesus willingly suffered and died in humiliation, but He did so at the *heavenly Father's* request as part of an ingenious plan to secure *our* redemption.

How we define our individual identities begins with how we perceive our heavenly Father. This is why we must learn to understand and trust the Bible. As the Holy Spirit opens our eyes to an accurate understanding of the Scriptures, we come to know in our hearts that God wants only the best for us, that He seeks to remove our shame regardless of its source, and that He will be the perfect Father even when our earthly examples fall woefully short.

It makes perfect sense that dark forces of evil would work nonstop to discredit the concept of fatherhood, and especially the stellar character of our heavenly Father. If we think Him to be distant, callous, vindictive, or abusive, we will never develop an accurate perspective of ourselves. As a painful consequence, we will stay mired in the depths of sin. Let us remember that our significance has nothing to do with how we feel but with how much He values us.

QUESTIONS

1. How has our perspective of fatherhood been distorted?

2. How are our perceptions of the heavenly Father and our sense of significance related?

3. Why does it matter that God loves us even when we are unworthy?

FURTHER READING: Isaiah 53 and 1 John 4:7–21

PRAYER: Heavenly Father, help me to know You as the perfectly loving Father You are, and help me to see myself the way You see me.

DAY TWENTY-FOUR
BECOMING A CHILD OF GOD

See how great a love the Father has bestowed on us, that we would be called children of God; and such we are.
1 John 3:1a

Why God should choose the meanest, basest, most unworthy individuals with absolutely nothing to commend them at all to God, except their miserable, lost condition, and then exalt them to become the sons of God, members of the divine family, and use them for His glory, is beyond all reason and human understanding. Yet that is grace.
—M. R. DeHaan

It was a typical day as I stood talking with a friend about important life issues such as trout fishing. What happened next, however, was anything but typical. A married couple—both in their forties—stopped and changed the flow of our conversation. Along with three kids (from elementary to high-school age) in tow, the father was also carrying an eight-week-old infant. The little boy came as a surprise at this stage of their lives, but not in the way one might expect.

Bill and Susie (as I will call them) had signed up to be foster parents and had requested an elementary-aged child. The agency was in a difficult situation, though, and asked if they would take a three-week-old infant. The birth mother was homeless and addicted, and the little guy still had drugs in his system. The father's situation was no better; his home had recently been condemned because of his own personal methamphetamine lab. Bill and Susie reluctantly agreed to take the baby.

During our conversation, the weary foster parents commented about how difficult it was in their stage in life to care for an infant—especially on such short notice, and with his challenges due to the lingering effects of narcotics. What I did not hear, however, were comments about wanting to get rid of the baby. In fact, Bill passionately proclaimed, "We're looking to adopt him. I couldn't imagine ever giving him up." After only five weeks, this child's name had been indelibly written on their hearts.

Many awe-inspiring expressions of love can be found in this world, but one of the most impressive is that of parents with their own natural children who choose to adopt. So much love fills their hearts that it cannot help but find expression in the life of a boy or girl who has no natural reason to enter their world.

The contrasts in an adopted child's life can be huge. He or she might go from being orphaned, neglected, or abused to becoming a cherished member of a healthy family; from being abandoned with no connections or privilege in life, to having an unearned sense of acceptance, significance, and security. Another family I know has added two special needs orphans from overseas to their already-full household. To go from being abandoned to becoming a deeply loved member of a healthy family—the contrast cannot be more extreme.

Considering the father heart of God and His amazing love, it is no surprise the Bible uses the language of being adopted and becoming children of God to help illustrate our Christian experience. Thankfully for us, the sovereign Lord is not a foster parent who is subject to the mercy of human institutions.

> He came to His own, and those who were His own did not receive Him. But as many as received Him, to them He gave the right to become children of God, even to those who believe in His name, who were born, not of blood nor of the will of the flesh nor of the will of man, but of God. John 1:11–13

It is both unlikely and surprising that the perfect and sovereign Creator of all things would invite us to become His children. From a theological perspective, people are by nature *enemies* of God (Romans 5:8). In the garden of Eden, the human race joined Lucifer's rebellious coup to overthrow the King of Glory and usurp His throne. As a result, every human heart intrinsically seeks to exalt itself and proclaim its own glorious supremacy.

I am not claiming that all humans despise the concept of a benevolent god. The majority of us take comfort in knowing that someone big and powerful is looking out for us in this crazy world. Thus, the general image of a god who calms our fears and serves our needs is quite palatable. What we tend to despise, though, is a *real* God who refuses to bow to our will or conform to our standards.

Humanity's "I will ascend" mentality generates never-ending competition for heaven's glorious throne. Whether we realize it or not, we are all born into this world with the innate desire to usurp the King of Glory and be crowned king or queen of the universe. And so it is that our ever-present human reality is one of pushing and shoving— and worse—as we continually vie for supremacy.

Amazingly, it was God the Father who "engineered" our redemption from this hopeless "I will ascend" cycle. Indeed, this is the message of the Christian gospel of grace. Though humans were created to be children of God, we broke ranks from His family in an attempt to gain self-exalting independence. In seeking to be like God apart from God, humanity joined a violent coup against the benevolent Creator of all things. Through a mysterious and unlikely plan, however, the heavenly Father then sent His beloved Son to suffer and die an excruciating death as the perfect sacrifice for our sins. Now, through faith in Christ and His redemptive work, the Father gives us the opportunity to be adopted as His royal children. What an amazing blessing at such a profound cost!

Until we become God's children through faith in Christ, we remain on the outside looking in, alienated from our Creator and devoid of lasting hope. In this sense, Christianity is *exclusive*: only through Jesus can we become members of God's household. At the same time, our heavenly Father reveals His *inclusive* love by inviting people of *all* backgrounds to join His family regardless of social sphere, ethnicity, or moral history.

While parental love and the legal nature of adoption are vastly important, there is a third component to the process that means everything: the child's *perception* of his or her status in the family. Regardless of how much they are loved by their adoptive parents, some children continue to struggle with rejection, haunted by the feeling that they were abandoned by their birth parents. Such a sense of "inglorious insecurity" then creates many of the problems described in Phase Two of this book.

Again, the parallel with our Christian experience is clear. If we, as the adopted children of the heavenly Father, fail to adequately perceive who He is, how much He loves us, and who we become in Him, we will remain mired in the glory-deficient mentalities of our old, fallen selves. If our quest for significance is defined by what we can accomplish rather than by our new identities in Christ, the shackles of sin will remain firmly clamped to our wrists. We will trudge through a burdened existence as slaves to approval rather than as free children of the living God.

The gospel is not just a message of future destiny, but also of present identity. Through the Father's unconditional love, Jesus' abundant grace, and the tender comfort of the Holy Spirit, you can discover your identity as God's child and break free from the superhero masks, protective fig leaves, and false facades that keep our world bound.

Do you realize the exorbitant price that God paid on your behalf? Can you grasp how much heartache you have caused Him? As weighty as these ideas are, neither is at the forefront of His mind. The heavenly Father loves you perfectly, and none of your shortcomings, failures, or problems can make Him love you less. He has indelibly written your name upon His heart, and He cannot imagine ever giving you up!

QUESTIONS

1. Why are humans innately enemies of God?

2. What makes adoption more a message of love than of rejection?

3. Why is it vital that we understand the gospel to be a message of present identity as much as that of a future destiny?

FURTHER READING: John 1:1-17 and Galatians 4:1-7

PRAYER: Heavenly Father, thank you so much for loving the entire human race despite our sins, and for saving a special place in your family just for me.

DAY TWENTY-FIVE
THE COVENANT FAMILY OF GOD

Jesus said, "Truly I say to you, there is no one who has left house or brothers or sisters or mother or father or children or farms, for My sake and for the gospel's sake, but that he will receive a hundred times as much now in the present age, houses and brothers and sisters and mothers and children and farms, along with persecutions; and in the age to come, eternal life."
Mark 10:29–30

We are adopted into God's family through the resurrection of Christ from the dead in which he paid all our obligations to sin, the law, and the devil, in whose family we once lived. Our old status lies in his tomb. A new status is ours through his resurrection.
—Sinclair B. Ferguson

On May 23, 1862, the United States Civil War battle of Front Royal (Virginia) was marked by a unique and peculiar event: the Union 1st Regiment Maryland Volunteer Infantry fought against the 1st Maryland Infantry, CSA of the Confederate Army. It was the only time in U.S. history when two regiments with the same numerical designation from the same state fought against one another on the battlefield.

How painfully confusing it must have been for friends and even family members to shoot, kill, and imprison one another. Even more interesting is the fact that Captain William Goldsborough of the Confederate army captured a Union prisoner who looked rather familiar: his own brother Charles!

Having won the war, the Northerners moved on with their lives. Yes, the presence of scarred bodies and the bitter loss of loved ones lingered for many decades, but victory also brought a kind of emotional vindication. Having grown up in rural Pennsylvania—a northern state—the Civil War was a non-issue for everyone I knew. Apart from visits to historic battlefields, no one gave it much thought.

When our class learned about the North-South conflict in the fifth grade, my friends and I took the keen sort of interest boys that age are inclined to take. Oblivious to the scope of pain involved with mortal combat, we chose sides and staged mock battles. But when that part of the history lesson came to an end, our interest evaporated, and we moved on with our focus.

Not until many years later did I realize how much the war and its causes still influenced both Southerners and African Americans. Southerners lost loved ones, wealth, and property in the conflict, and continue to view the war differently from Northerners to this day. African Americans lost lives, freedom, community, and homeland long before the war ever started, and continue to feel the effects of oppression in modern times.

The United States Civil War ended long ago, but the resulting emotional battles continue to rage because deep-rooted glory deficiencies have never been satisfied. This realization brings us to a powerful truth: *if a people's core identity is taken away, for them to be fully restored, a more significant one must be provided in return.* If not, the ensuing struggles will last for generations.

One of the new identities our Creator provides for us is to become part of the *family* of God, but that also presents a problem. In an ideal world, families are happy, wholesome, and supportive. Our real-life families can be a different story, however, as they often fall far short of our expectations—especially when two brothers fight on opposing sides of a civil war.

In multiple ways, the Christian church was meant to function as the family of God on this earth. Yet again, reality is far from the ideal. No doubt, the church is often criticized unjustly, but we would be foolish to deny the dysfunction that permeates so many of our local fellowships. Far too many of us have been deeply wounded by attitudes and actions that should never exist among God's people.

A major part of our problem results from our ignorance regarding God's design for the family. Ancient historical records from across the globe speak of a concept that has been largely lost to contemporary Western culture: the *covenant*. A covenant is a sacred and legally binding relationship of the highest order. Covenants were—and are—so valued in some cultures that the worst sin against society would be to violate a covenant bond.

An appropriate illustration of a covenant might be a tight-knit military unit. When the U.S. Marines, for example, vow to leave no man behind, a covenant mindset is at work. Furthermore, this brotherhood mentality is sacrificially expressed on the battlefield when an individual risks his or her life for the sake of a wounded comrade.

Even a casual perusal of the Bible reveals the central role that covenants played in its redemptive story. In fact, entering into a sacred covenant with God is what set His people apart from all other nations on earth. They were "the people of the covenant."

If I could use one phrase to describe a covenantal mindset, it would be "faithful love." I am tempted to use "extremely faithful love," for emphasis, but that would be inaccurate. A husband, for example, cannot be extremely faithful to his wife. He is either faithful or he is not. If he sleeps with a woman other than his spouse even once, he has been unfaithful.

The love-motivated faithfulness of a covenant relationship provides a visual representation of God's faithfulness toward His children. Our heavenly Father is not "extremely faithful," He is *faithful*. Period. His loving devotion to His children is unwavering. There has never been—and never will be—a time when the Lord has been unfaithful.

Those who enter into the new covenant through faith in Jesus Christ become full-fledged members of God's royal household. They become "princes" and "princesses," if you will. *The revelation that we are cherished members of God's royal family is an eternal truth that forms the core essence of our identities, far surpassing gender, race, nationality, or any other natural source of significance.*

The new covenant, which places a higher emphasis on our common identities as God's children than on natural distinctions, provides the most effective way to foster true and lasting healing between opposing groups. When we learn to elevate and celebrate our sacred bond as brothers and sisters in Christ, issues such as skin color, ethnicity, and denomination lose their power to divide.

God's devotion is to *His children*, not just to any individual child. He loves each with equal passion and equal faithfulness. It also means that *when we enter into a new covenant relationship with Christ, we enter into a covenant relationship with all of God's children.* This royal family of the King of kings and Lord of lords is of the highest eternal order.

It should be no surprise that the Christian church has been as caustically maligned as our images of both fatherhood and of the heavenly Father Himself. The dark forces of hell wage an endless campaign to portray that which is glorious as shameful. Regardless of human and demonic smear campaigns, however, the covenant people of God belong to one glorious and profoundly beautiful family. The process is often messy, but despite often shallow faith, hypocritical actions, and institutionalized religion, the true family of God is growing into the likeness of Jesus.

As the upheaval in our world seems to increase, and as earthly institutions continue to shake, the reality of being members of God's household must grow in our hearts. The Bible is full of covenantal promises which have given His children strength, stability, and hope through some of the worst circumstances imaginable. The blessed combination of knowing our elite standing as the covenant children of God, along with the heavenly Father's faithful character, gives us strength in hard times and helps us develop an unwavering sense of identity.

QUESTIONS

1. Why is a covenant much more than simply an agreement?

2. How do covenants in the Bible help portray God's faithfulness to His children?

3. What does it mean to be a part of the covenant family of God?

FURTHER READING: Genesis 15 and Hebrews 8

PRAYER: Heavenly Father, please help me grasp both the wisdom and security of covenant faithfulness.

DAY TWENTY-SIX
CHOSEN BY GOD

Blessed be the God and Father of our Lord Jesus Christ, who has blessed us with every spiritual blessing in the heavenly places in Christ, just as He chose us in Him before the foundation of the world that we would be holy and blameless before Him.

Ephesians 1:3–4a

There are two great truths which from this platform I have proclaimed for many years. The first is that salvation is free to every man who will have it; the second is that God gives salvation to a people whom He has chosen; and these truths are not in conflict with each other in the least degree.

—Charles Spurgeon

Have you ever contemplated the extent of the universe? It takes only a picture or two from deep space to humble my intellectual pride and enamor me with the mystery of our grand cosmos. In particular, I sometimes wonder what is to be found at the edge of the universe. All I can envision is a towering red-brick wall. But if such a wall did happen to exist, my next thought would then be, "I wonder what is on the other side." The idea of a brick wall is ludicrous, but an intellectually honest person cannot help but admit that human comprehension is woefully limited in light of our seemingly infinite cosmos.

Just as the magnitude of our universe remains unfathomable, so is the immenseness of God. Our Creator is infinite and self-existent, while we are finite and dependent creatures. As amazing as our intellectual capacities might be, it is impossible for humanity to even begin to grasp all He is, or all He knows.

From a theological perspective, one issue confounding us most involves the relationship between *our human free will* and *God's sovereign authority*. For centuries, a "theological war" has raged between those who champion one viewpoint over the other. I think both sides are partly correct and partly wrong at the same time.

Strange as it might seem, both arguments find solid Biblical support. A thoughtful reader can just as easily uncover passages emphasizing God's sovereign influence on human decisions as those asserting our freedom to make choices. Gathering an array of Bible verses, proponents of either position can build theological constructs to support their perspectives. The problem is that they have to ignore—or theologically twist—those passages that fail to conform to their preferred narrative.

I have chosen to resolve the issue of God's sovereignty versus human free will by not resolving it. In essence, I do not believe we can draw a clear line between divine sovereignty and human freedom. Instead, an element of mystery will always permeate the issue. Admittedly, I lean toward emphasizing human free will, but not to the exclusion of God's unmatched power. The King of Glory, you see, is sovereign. He is the highest and most powerful authority in the universe. No one can limit His authority or call Him into account. God does what He pleases, and thankfully, what He pleases is always motivated by love.

With wisdom beyond our comprehension, our sovereign Lord chose to create humans in His image. In doing so, He gave us the innate capacity to love, and thus, the freedom to make our own choices. This freedom is powerfully illustrated by the two trees—the tree of life and the tree of the knowledge of good and evil—that He placed at the center of Eden's garden. Despite innocent blood spilled and horrible atrocities committed, as long as we walk this earth, God will never take away our freedom to choose.

By giving us free will, our Creator did nothing to limit His own authority. Instead, through His all-powerful ability, the Almighty God turns even our free choices toward His divine purposes. How does He do this? We are clueless. At least in part, this is what makes Him *God*. Humans are prone to controlling others, but the Lord accomplishes His purposes by influencing without controlling, without violating our freedom of choice. Such a perspective presents a far higher view of God's sovereignty than that of a giant "puppet master" in the heavens who controls everyone's actions through a preprogrammed performance.

Considering all these things, only with a profound sense of mystery do I address the issue of predestination and being chosen by God. I will not try to draw a line between God's part and our part, but simply appreciate the reality of being chosen by Him for what it is: weighty and amazing, far beyond our comprehension.

Our world's philosophy for choosing people is *value-driven*. Growing up, for example, I was no athletic wonder. My classmates reminded me of this sad reality every time they picked teams in gym class. The teacher would choose the two best athletes to be the team captains. Those two would then pick, one by one, the remaining class members in order of their perceived ability. The worst were picked last, and in junior high, I was rightly reckoned to be among the dregs of athletic society. Thus, I was chosen for a team only when the superstar captains had come down to their final options.

When it comes to God's "team," the scenario is quite different. The sovereign Lord chooses people because *He wants to*, and why He wants to often makes no logical sense to us. Furthermore, God's choice is intentional. He never acts because of limited options but because He chooses to express His love in mysterious ways.

The person who genuinely comes to Christ does not do so because he or she suddenly decides that it is a good idea to pursue spiritual things. Instead, before the Lord set into motion the creation of our world, and before the human race spoiled the paradise of Eden, God chose you and me for adoption into His family. Being chosen by God before the foundation of the world can be likened to being picked first in gym class, but for much different reasons, and on a far grander scale.

Why does the heavenly Father choose a person for His royal family? Because He wants to. We can attempt to identify this or that reason, but in the end, our explanations ring hollow. One thing remains for sure: our selection has *nothing* to do with what we have to offer. Our Lord often reveals His glorious handiwork by accomplishing the most with the least (1 Corinthians 1:26–29). The true brilliance of His glory will be revealed only through humble human vessels.

In Ephesians 1:4, Paul proclaimed that the heavenly Father "chose us in Him before the foundation of the world." In fact, most of that chapter celebrates all of the good that God has done for His children. The learned apostle seemed more inclined to express wonder over the issue of sovereignty and free will than to argue about an elusive line of separation (see Romans 11).

God creating us in His image means not only that He wanted us to be like Him, but also that He wanted us from the beginning. And Jesus paying the extreme price of suffering and death on the cross to make us children of God indicates that He wanted us—and continues to want us—despite our sins and failures.

Rejection often overwhelms our hearts with sad and forlorn "ichabod emotions." But the feeling of being chosen is quite the opposite. How our spirits soar with a profound sense of significance when we are chosen! And how much more meaningful it is to be handpicked by the exalted King of Glory!

Regardless of how loudly the voices of this world criticize, belittle, or condemn, *the sovereign King of kings and Lord of lords has chosen you to be a cherished member of His royal family!* Can you imagine a more glorious or greater honor? None exists. How will you choose to respond to His mysterious love?

QUESTIONS

1. In what ways do we err when we argue about God's sovereignty versus human free will?

2. Why is it vital to understand that being chosen by God has nothing to do with our own merits?

3. How does the idea of being chosen by God make you feel?

FURTHER READING: Romans 11 and Ephesians 1:3–14

PRAYER: Sovereign Lord, I do not understand why You did so, but I thank You for choosing me!

DAY TWENTY-SEVEN
THE APPLE OF HIS EYE

―――――◗◉◖―――――

I will make you into a great nation,
I will bless you,
I will make your name great,
and you will be a blessing.
I will bless those who bless you,
I will curse those who treat you with contempt,
and all the peoples on earth
will be blessed through you.
Genesis 12:2–3 (HCSB)

I am graven on the palms of His hands. I am never out of His mind. All my knowledge of Him depends on His sustained initiative in knowing me. I know Him, because He first knew me, and continues to know me. He knows me as a friend, One who loves me; and there is no moment when His eye is off me, or His attention distracted for me, and no moment, therefore, when His care falters.
—J. I. Packer

Roughly four thousand years ago, the Creator of our cosmos did something unthinkable: He initiated a sacred and binding covenant with a human. That man's name was *Abram*, whom God later renamed *Abraham*.

In this covenant relationship, God expected Abraham to be "all in." The man was to surrender everything he held dear to the Lord's will. In return, He promised Abraham significance and greatness. This promise was unsolicited; God destined greatness for Abraham and his descendants without being asked. I also find the first part of Genesis 12:3 to be especially telling:

> I will bless those who bless you,
> I will curse those who treat you with contempt. (HCSB)

This passage stretches the boundaries of our comprehension. The Almighty declared that He would relate to people based on how they related to Abraham. Those who blessed the man would be blessed, and those who so much as treated Abraham with contempt would have curses heaped upon their heads. What does this tell us? To the Creator of all things, Abraham was one special guy, *the apple of His eye*, if you will.

What did Abraham do to earn such privileged status? Nothing. God conceived a plan before the foundation of the world that, for reasons beyond our grasp, involved making Abraham the point man. But it was not just about one person. The Lord intended to use Abraham and his progeny to bless all the peoples of the earth.

God rarely acts according to human expectations, and the situation with Abraham's descendants was no different. Specifically, when Jesus initiated the new covenant some 2,000 years later, Abraham's lineage became one of *faith* and not human DNA.

> Just as Abraham believed God, and it was credited to him for righteousness, then understand that those who have faith are Abraham's sons. Now the Scripture saw in advance that God would justify the Gentiles by faith and told the good news ahead of time to Abraham, saying, All the nations will be blessed through you. So those who have faith are blessed with Abraham, who had faith. Galatians 3:6–9 (HCSB)

Paul's point is significant. The covenant God made with Abraham is fulfilled in every person who becomes a Christian through faith in Jesus. The majority of the promises found in the Bible were made to His covenant people, and the full promise of God's devotion now belongs to us, regardless of how inglorious we might think we are.

To feel like an Ichabod is common in a world that values people for what they can offer. Feelings of insignificance and abandonment can arise in our hearts as quickly as a thunderstorm on a hot summer's day. Throughout the centuries, generations of God's people have wrestled with the notion of the heavenly Father's favor despite our weaknesses and shortcomings.

The following dialogue recorded by Isaiah the prophet provides a powerful reminder of the Lord's covenant faithfulness:

> But Zion said, "The Lord has forsaken me,
> And the Lord has forgotten me."
> "Can a woman forget her nursing child
> And have no compassion on the son of her womb?
> Even these may forget, but I will not forget you.
> Behold, I have inscribed you on the palms of My hands."
> Isaiah 49:14–16a

Do you see it? God told His covenant people that He had carved them into the palms of His hands. Their very identity was inexplicably linked to His own. All genuine Christians are the covenant children of the heavenly Father, and so this same notion applies to us as well.

To most parents, these ideas make perfect sense. From even before their births, our children have held a special place in the center of our hearts. It did not matter if they were surrounded by a sea of humanity; when the Santos kids participated in school events, our attention riveted on them. After all, they were our offspring who proceeded from our bodies and in our genetic likeness.

As deep as our love for our offspring runs, there is a heavenly Father whose devotion to His covenant children far surpasses that of the most stellar human parents. Consider the psalmist's revelation regarding God's heart toward him:

> How precious are your thoughts about me, O God.
>   They cannot be numbered!
> I can't even count them;
>   they outnumber the grains of sand!
> And when I wake up, you are still with me!
> Psalm 139:17–18 (NLT)

Can you accept that this passage also describes how the heavenly Father feels about you? It does not matter what struggles you face or how absent the Lord might seem. A person cannot begin to count all the grains of sand on this earth, nor can we fathom the degree to which we capture our heavenly Father's affections. *God's good desires for you are immeasurable!*

Even if you have experienced more than your share of mistreatment and abuse, you are *not* in the least desirable position. That inglorious state belongs to those who have treated you with contempt. As a child of God, you are Abraham's descendant and the apple of your heavenly Father's eye. He has inscribed your name on the palms of His hands, and He continually seeks the very best for your life. You are honored and blessed, regardless of how you feel.

Do not underestimate the fierceness of the Father's love for His covenant children. No doubt, there are times in the midst of our struggles when God might seem to be distant or uncaring; however, nothing of the sort is true. He is always close by, patiently watching, waiting, and working behind the scenes to arrange circumstances, situations, and provision for the benefit of those He loves.

Abraham was our forerunner in more ways than one, and we cannot miss this vital fact: he realized the fullness of the Father's blessings only *after* his faith had been tested, tried, and proven. If it is by faith that we become Abraham's descendants, it is also by faith that we realize the fullness of God's sweet blessings. Our circumstances sometimes feel dreadful, yet the Father's heart still beats with fierce love for His covenant children even on the darkest of days.

QUESTIONS

1. Why is it incredible that God makes covenants with humans?

2. What are the implications of being in a sacred covenant with God?

3. Why is it vital that we trust God's Word over our feelings?

FURTHER READING: Psalm 139:1–18 and Romans 8:28–39

PRAYER: Heavenly Father, please open my eyes to Your love and help me to realize my significance as the apple of Your eye.

DAY TWENTY-EIGHT
INTIMACY WITH GOD

"This is eternal life, that they may know You, the only true God, and Jesus Christ whom You have sent."
John 17:3

It seems to me, as time goes on, that the only thing that is worth seeking for is to know and to be known by Christ—a privilege open alone to the childlike, who, with receptivity, guilelessness, and humility, move Godward.
—Charles H. Brent

Not long ago, I stopped at a local Catholic church for their annual used book sale. This event draws large crowds of people from all walks of life because of the large number of books available. On the day I visited, the religion section alone consisted of fifteen long tables covered with books. The vast majority of those works were Christian, and their hundreds of titles covered everything from discovering purpose in life, to instructions on prayer, to finding peace in our present age.

A series of observations and thoughts began flowing through my mind as I looked for hidden gems with titles that caught my interest. Near me was a middle-aged man whose arms strained from the weight of a growing number of volumes. A couple of his titles looked helpful, but I had significant doubts about several more.

Our world abounds with knowledge, only a portion of which is both accurate and meaningful. The Bible tells us that some people will spend their entire lives learning without ever coming to a realization of the truth (2 Timothy 3:1-7). Even acquiring vast amounts of knowledge about God does not equate to *knowing* Him. Accumulating information is one thing, but knowing Him in our hearts and spirits is another matter entirely.

Herein lies the difference between "head knowledge" and "heart knowledge." Head knowledge enables us to *know about* a person, but heart knowledge involves actually *knowing* that individual. Throughout the centuries, vast numbers of religious people have known about God while lacking an actual relationship with Him.

The contrast between head knowledge and heart knowledge was illustrated in the life of Will—a young man whom I have known for several years. Will had been heavily involved in a local Bible-believing church and had shown a seemingly genuine devotion to the Lord. In fact, I was secretly embarrassed (it is no secret now!) when Will and his friend attended a Bible study I was leading. Having put considerable time and effort into memorizing the Scriptures, they recited verse after verse during our discussion. I have several passages memorized, but I am more of a concept person, and so I felt somewhat inferior in light of their surpassing ability to speak from memory so much of God's sacred Word. Still, something about Will seemed off. His zeal for spiritual matters was admirable, but his faith seemed rigid or sterile, almost like a duty, and unlike what one would expect to see in a natural relationship.

We fell out of touch and then reconnected two or three years later. Even in light of my previous concerns, the story Will told caught me by surprise. The young man had gone through a long, painful period in which he had lost all sense of his spiritual and emotional bearings. Nothing he did, including reciting Bible verses, seemed to help during that time of intense internal distress.

Eventually, Will came to the point of admitting his inability to please God and began the journey to a fully surrendered life. From that point on, his life began to change dramatically. To my surprise, Will was convinced that he did not even become a Christian until he began to make that full and fresh surrender to the Lord.

Regardless of when the young man became a genuine believer, Will's story echoes a profound truth: *a person can be well-versed in the Bible, and even highly knowledgeable about God, without actually knowing God.*

In the Gospel that bears his name, the apostle John records the final thoughts Jesus shared with his disciples just prior to the cross (John 13–17). Virtually all scholars agree that these last words carry special weight as the Son of Man put the finishing touches on his ministry. Do you know what is one of the most—if not the most—predominant themes in this section of Scripture? Relational intimacy between God and His children.

These five chapters of John's gospel are replete with words and phrases such as "know," "abide," "disclose," "become one with," and "be with you forever." As He wrapped up His ministry on earth, Jesus emphasized knowing God and relating to other Christians. Why would He do that? *The Son of God chose to shine a spotlight on the very reason for which He came: the restoration of relational intimacy between humans and their Creator.*

In the garden of Eden, Adam and Eve walked with God until they were ejected for joining Lucifer's cosmic rebellion. Then, during Old Testament times, the Lord's presence dwelt in the midst of His people, but only a few (i.e., the priests) had direct access. Today, we are under the new covenant in Christ. As a result of Jesus' sacrifice, God's presence, through the person of the Holy Spirit, dwells within the heart of every true Christian. The word *gospel* means "good news," and there is no better news than that which announces our undeserved opportunity to continually dwell in the presence of the King of Glory.

Through the unlikely death and subsequent resurrection of Jesus, the Creator of the Universe did what He always seems to do: turned the worst imaginable situation into unimaginable blessings. As amazing as the paradise of Eden might have been, heaven will be so much greater. Eternal life, however, does not just begin in heaven—it begins *in this life* as we develop an intimate relationship with the heavenly Father (John 17:3). The exciting reality of intimacy with God was emphasized not only by John, but by Paul as well:

> But when the fullness of the time came, God sent forth His Son, born of a woman, born under the Law, so that He might redeem those who were under the Law, that we might receive the adoption as sons [used in a generic sense for both men and women]. Because you are sons, God has sent forth the Spirit of His Son into our hearts, crying, "Abba! Father!" Galatians 4:4–6

The word *abba* is a term for father—used here with intimacy and endearment. What makes this passage especially interesting is the role the Holy Spirit plays in our relationship with the heavenly Father. Much like an affectionate mother encouraging the bonding between infant and father, the Holy Spirit speaks to our hearts the message: "That's your *Abba*, you know. That's your *Abba*. He loves you so much. He would go to the ends of the earth for you."

The message of intimately knowing the heavenly Father is not only sweet news for the human soul, it also has a profoundly practical effect. As our glory deficiencies are satisfied by the glory that emanates from our majestic King, our human dysfunction will begin to dissipate. True glory satisfies the soul and severs the roots that divide us, thereby setting the stage for healthier relationships not only with the Lord, but also with other humans. Only through the glory of the Almighty's presence can we navigate the ever-elusive path to interpersonal harmony.

Adam and Eve ate from the tree of the knowledge of good and evil with the desire to know everything there is to know, but independent from God. The Old Testament law allowed people to relate to God, but only from a distance. Jesus then came to show us that the essence of life is to know God intimately. *The continued presence of the Holy Spirit in our hearts means that the Lord will be ever near, and I cannot think of anything more meaningful.*

QUESTIONS

1. What is the difference between knowing God and simply knowing about God?

2. What enables us to have an intimate relationship with God?

3. Why must our glory deficiencies be satisfied for our earthly relationships to be healthy?

FURTHER READING: John 16:5–15 and John 17

PRAYER: Lord, please help me not just to know *about* You, but to *know* You intimately!

DAY TWENTY-NINE
NEW CREATURES IN CHRIST

Therefore from now on we recognize no one according to the flesh; even though we have known Christ according to the flesh, yet now we know Him in this way no longer. Therefore if anyone is in Christ, he is a new creature; the old things passed away; behold, new things have come.
2 Corinthians 5:16–17

The Spiritual Life is the gift of the Living Spirit. The spiritual man is no mere development of the natural man. He is a New Creation born from Above.
—Henry Drummond

Debi and I lived in a university community (aka "a college town") for much of our adult lives. And while I do not appreciate ear-popping music and three-day-long parties, there were aspects of life in a college town that expanded our horizons. Over the years, our local university enrolled hundreds of international students from all over the globe. On any given day, we would see people from Asia, India, or the Middle East—an uncommon diversity for many rural American communities. These individuals added flavor to our small town, and getting to know some of them greatly enlarged our perspective of the world.

Sometimes our relationships with international students began spontaneously, and other times Debi and I reached out through a university host-family program. Regardless of how the connections came to be, we found the vast majority favorable.

Being the host-country citizens, rarely were we in the minority. I did experience a couple of occasions, however, when I felt like a foreigner in my own homeland. One of these times was when I drove a Chinese student to the Pittsburgh airport to pick up his wife.

Several of Limin's acquaintances joined us, and of our merry group of eight, I was the lone non-Chinese member.

Even more interesting was stopping at a Chinese restaurant on the way home. I could not understand a single word of the fast-paced dialogue. "What did the restaurant manager say to you?" I asked. My friend responded, "Oh, she said not to get the wonton soup. It is Americanized and not very good."

On another occasion, I was invited to a local mosque as the annual Ramadan fast was coming to an end. There I sat with a room full of Arabic men and boys, eating dates and feeling clueless about the conversations ebbing and flowing around me. When we moved to a different room so that they could recite their prayers, I sat in the back and quietly prayed to the heavenly Father.

None of the men were light skinned like me, and they prayed in Arabic. Furthermore, the mosque differed significantly from my church—we all sat on the floor to eat—and the food was Middle Eastern (and delicious). Most certainly, in these situations, I felt like an outsider.

Feeling like a foreigner in a familiar land was a theme that the writer of Hebrews addressed when he referred to heroes of the faith as "strangers and exiles" on earth (Hebrews 11:13-16). This statement seems somewhat bizarre because earth is where they had always lived. Their citizenship, however, was of a *heavenly country*.

The train of thought from Hebrews 11:13-16 aligns well with that of the apostle Paul's who called us "new creatures" in Christ (2 Corinthians 5:17). Paul was not emphasizing the fact that we are creatures, but that we are a *new* kind of creature, unlike anything that has existed before. To better grasp Paul's meaning, we must begin with Adam and end with Jesus.

When Adam and Eve violated the only rule of Eden by eating from the tree of the knowledge of good and evil, something terrible happened; their spirits died to God. Not only were they separated from His presence, they could no longer know Him intimately. Nor could they live with the spiritual vitality needed to reign over dark thoughts and selfish motives.

Herein lies a Biblical truth that many people ignore to their own detriment: *spiritual death is the natural, default state for all humans.*

Unless we are "born again"—or "born from above"—we cannot see God's kingdom or know His ways (John 3:3). Thus, while the ideals of the Christian faith appeal to the multitudes, only a few can grasp a practical understanding of its dynamics.

When we believe in Christ and subsequently receive Him as Lord and Savior, something beyond magical takes place. God, through the presence of the Holy Spirit, enters our previously dead spirit and brings it to life. Our newly vitalized human spirit, which is mysteriously intertwined with God Himself, is unlike any other creature. We are aware of no other life form in the universe that is born into sin's death and then brought spiritually alive by an "imperishable seed" (1 Peter 1:23).

Strangely enough, because this God-initiated transformation is spiritual, a person's outward appearance might not change all that much. A newly "reborn" Christian can still live in the same neighborhood, wear the same clothes, and eat the same food as always. Spiritual perspectives and thought patterns, however, are a different matter.

Before I became a Christian, I pretty much thought and acted like my peers. After being adopted into the family of God, I became an "oddball" (at least, more than my usual strange self). For example, getting drunk no longer appealed to me, and the quest to make a name for myself began to lose its allure. Perhaps most significant of all, the way I viewed other people changed. The divisions—gender, race, ethnicity—which stratify so many cultures began to fade. Albeit slowly, I started to see people not for these characteristics, but as image-bearers of God.

With this transformation taking place within my own heart, I began to feel like a foreigner in my own land. My perspectives, my desires, and my words—all began to change and differ from the world I had called "home" since the day of my birth. And if trying to fit in felt difficult before, it now seemed impossible. Furthermore, those old identifiers—the labels that make people feel significant—suddenly seemed like shallow and temporary facades, unable to bear the weight of true and lasting significance.

In becoming a new creature, I had taken on a new identity. No longer defined by natural characteristics such as gender, race, and nationality, my intimate association with the King of Glory became the mark that made me significant—even as I became more of an Ichabod in the eyes of my peers.

We need to be sure of our identities in the eyes of God because identifying with Him *will* make us strangers to popular culture. The world despises those who march to the beat of a heavenly Drummer, who refuse to conform to social pressures. If human approval drives us, we will lose much. We will lose vitality. We will lose purpose. We will lose those identifiers intended by God to make us unique. Worse still, we will stray from our Lord's design and forfeit our opportunity to influence the other inhabitants of this planet.

I see no need to abandon the sources of diversity that help keep life interesting, but our new identity in Christ must be our primary focus. Natural identifiers should always place a distant second. Heaven will one day be filled with diverse peoples from all over this pale blue dot we call "Planet Earth." Gender, skin color, nationality—if these characteristics mean anything in the next life, they will only add color and flavor; they will not divide us.

We do not need to wait for eternity to see peace among humans. We can make our common identities as children of God our primary focus today. *By living out transformative lives as new creatures in Him, we can help return the paradise that was lost to this earth.* Current and future generations will all benefit!

QUESTIONS

1. Think about a time when being a follower of Jesus made you feel like a stranger in a foreign land. How did you respond?

2. What does it mean to be a new creature in Christ?

3. Why is it vital that we become firmly established in our new identity in Christ?

FURTHER READING: Colossians 3:1–17 and Hebrews 11:1–16

PRAYER: Lord, please help me to fully embrace and live out my new identity in You.

DAY THIRTY
NEVER ABANDONED

Surely goodness and lovingkindness will follow me all the days of my life,
And I will dwell in the house of the Lord forever.

Psalm 23:6

God is faithful even when his children are not.

—Max Lucado

"Tap! Tap! Tap!" The sound of leathery knuckles rapping on the van window startled me to attention. A few inches away, on the other side of that thin glass, stood the imposing figure of a husky Native American man carrying a knapsack filled with *dream catchers*—wooden hoops beautifully decorated with cloth and feathers. Cautiously, I rolled down the window as the smell of alcohol billowed into my nostrils.

"Hello!" the boisterous voice proclaimed. "My name is Chief Joseph, and I am a fourth-generation descendant of Sitting Bull. I am also an artist, and to welcome you to Rosebud, I would like to offer you a special deal on my handcrafted wares. Besides, I need money to buy groceries and gas." Thus began one of the more interesting experiences of my life on this earth.

The story started with a trip sponsored by our church to assist the work of a missionary couple among the Lakota Sioux people of the Rosebud Indian Reservation. With a nice mix of children and adults, we had driven two fifteen-passenger vans filled with people, luggage, and tools from Western Pennsylvania to the beautiful landscape of South Dakota.

One of our projects involved cutting much-needed firewood to help several widows through the harsh temperatures and blustery winds of the upcoming winter. Upon starting his chainsaw, my friend

John soon realized that the blade was woefully dull. Unfortunately, one of his friends was not very sharp either.

Popping the van's hood to access its battery, John began to show me how to sharpen the chain. Keen with interest, I unwittingly rested my right hand on the van. Then it happened! Without warning, a large gust of wind blew out of nowhere. Down crashed the van hood, latching tight over the engine and trapping my fingers between the metal!

Writhing in pain, I jumped from one foot to the other (my friends gave me the name "Dances with Hoods"), unable to free myself from my predicament. After taking a long nap—or so it seemed—John finally opened the van door, released the hood latch, and pried the heavy sheet metal off my bloodied fingers. Thankfully, no bones were broken; however, the shreds of skin hanging from three of my fingers made it obvious that stitches would be needed. That is how I found myself sitting in the front seat of a fifteen-passenger van staring at blood-soaked paper towels while another friend (Kim) inquired to see if the reservation clinic would treat my wounds.

I did not buy any wares from Chief Joseph, and I did not give him any cash, but after having my fingers stitched, Kim and I purchased enough groceries for him to fill a shopping cart. We then drove Joseph home. It had taken our missionary hosts two years to be invited into a Native American home, but there we sat, welcomed guests in Chief Joseph's house after only two days in that territory.

As our Native American host shared about his tumultuous life, it became obvious that I was not the only one with painful wounds. Many years prior, Joseph and his spouse had been actively involved with Christian ministry. (He played us a recording of his own gospel music.) Sadly, Joseph's wife and his best friend had an affair and ran off together, leaving the once-vibrant man broken and alone. Bitterness set in, and alcohol became his intimate friend. Neither the passage of time nor the power of liquor had alleviated the wounded man's pain.

As we sat in his living room and talked, Joseph gratefully exclaimed, "I want to give you a gift!" In a matter of seconds, I was holding a huge buffalo skull brightly decorated with spiritual markings. At that moment, I did something our missionary hosts had told us never to do; I refused a gift from a Native American.

"I cannot accept this item," I replied. "The markings are of a spiritual nature, and I believe they conflict with my Christian faith." Startled and offended, Joseph stepped back and began an angry diatribe about the white man's God and the oppression of his people. With equal boldness (which was somewhat out of character for me), I patiently but firmly explained that God was not the God of white people only, but of all nations, tribes, and tongues (see Revelation 7:9–10). Furthermore, the injustices done against Native Americans might have been done in the name of God, but they violated His loving will.

The tension evaporated as quickly as it had begun, and our conversation returned to a calm demeanor. My host then offered me the gift of an inexpensive picture hanging on the wall, which I graciously accepted. It was not the item of value that he had wanted to share, but the thoughtfulness of the gesture was understood by both parties.

The story did not end there, however, as I steered our conversation back to the pain of his betrayal and the bitterness in his heart. We talked about the need to let go and forgive, about how it would help to restore his walk with God and bring healing to his own life. That led to a heartfelt prayer through which Chief Joseph verbally forgave both his ex-wife and former best friend.

The following year, Kim returned to the Rosebud Reservation with another group from our church. High on her agenda was reconnecting with Joseph and his family. She was disappointed to hear that he had passed away that winter from liver disease.

Our experience with Chief Joseph had a significant influence on me for two primary reasons. First, it provided a reminder that not every bad experience I face is about me. I cannot say that God caused that gust of wind to slam the van hood down on my fingers—I bear on my body the brand marks of my own stupidity—but I do know that He uses the pain of His covenant children for the benefit of others. This fact perturbs me at times, but in the end, I would not have it any other way.

Second, I saw with my own eyes how much the heavenly Father pursues those who are a part of His covenant family. It had probably been four decades since Joseph had walked away from the Lord, wrongly blaming Him for the betrayal committed by two selfish humans. But the Lord never forgot His wayward child. Just before the man's death, He sent two bumbling people (okay, maybe only one of us was a bumbler) halfway across the United States to help nudge Joseph back into the Shepherd's fold.

The Lord is faithful in ways that stretch our human intellects. When David the shepherd penned in Psalm 23:6, "Surely goodness and lovingkindness will follow me all the days of my life," he was reflecting on the heart of the Good Shepherd who will go to the ends of the earth—and send his children there as well—on behalf of a wayward sheep.

Adverse circumstances might tempt us to believe that we are all alone in a world spinning out of control. Add to that feelings of guilt and condemnation from falling prey to the enticements of sin, and we can easily begin to feel that God has abandoned us. *However, no amount of ugly human behavior can alter the depth of our Savior's unconditional and faithful love.* We might abandon God, but He will *never* abandon His beloved children!

QUESTIONS

1. Why is abandonment such a huge fear for many of us?

2. What does it mean to say that God is faithful to His covenant children?

3. Why is it shortsighted to be self-centered in our trials?

FURTHER READING: Luke 15:11–32 and 2 Timothy 2:8–13

PRAYER: Good Shepherd, I thank You that You will never fail or forsake me. Please help me to be ever faithful to You.

PHASE THREE REFLECTIONS

It is nothing short of amazing that the Creator of our vast cosmos chose to fashion humanity in His image. Our world often values people based on what they have to offer, but God takes a radically different approach. Every human life explodes with significance at the realization that our individual worth is not earned but given freely by the King of Glory. (Day 21)

Not only did God create us in His image, Jesus also descended from heaven and conformed Himself to our human image. He did this so that He might identify with the depths of our shame and give us the opportunity to identify with the heights of His glory. No greater measure of selfless love has ever been displayed to our ego-driven species. (Day 22)

Far too many people fail to experience the power of God's unconditional love. In large part, this is because much of Western culture has wrongly maligned the concept of fatherhood, which negatively affects our perception of the heavenly Father. Since our identities are based upon our relational connection with the heavenly Father, how we perceive Him greatly affects our sense of security. Only as we come to recognize, value, and appreciate the depth of God's amazing love, will we find security in His strong and faithful arms. (Day 23)

One of the most profound truths of the Bible tells us that the heavenly Father wants to adopt us into His royal family even though we were once His enemies. The Christian gospel is not just a message of future destiny, but also of present identity. If we want to break free from the power of sin, we must learn to establish a secure identity in and through Jesus. (Day 24)

Becoming a child of God involves entering into a special covenant with Him. A covenant is a sacred and binding relationship that is defined by faithful love. Entering into the new covenant through Jesus Christ sets us apart from all others on this earth, and the King of Glory's royal household forms the highest order of family imaginable. (Day 25)

Why we are chosen by God to be cherished members of His royal family is one of the great mysteries of the universe. We may never understand the complexities of human free will and God's divine providence, but we can focus on what we do know: the King of Glory has chosen us even though we were once His enemies. This incredible truth is worth celebrating! (Day 26)

The heavenly Father's love for His children is never casual or faltering. Instead, His eye watches over us with the faithful love of the most devoted parent. No matter what our circumstances might seem to be saying, the Lord will never forget or forsake His beloved children even on the darkest of days. (Day 27)

One of the many privileges of becoming a child of God is the opportunity to develop an intimate relationship with Him. There is a massive difference between knowing about God and actually knowing Him. The presence of the Holy Spirit living in our hearts allows us to know God intimately because He is always with us in the nearest way possible. (Day 28)

When we are born again (born from above) through the presence of the Holy Spirit, we become new creatures in Christ. Our new identities as the spiritual children of God then take precedence over natural attributes such as gender, race, or nationality. By focusing on our common identities as His children, we are unified as God's people and empowered to create lasting change, bringing love and peace to a world in need. (Day 29)

Our heavenly Father is faithful to His covenant children in a way that stretches beyond our human comprehension. He is the Good Shepherd who will never abandon His children. No matter how others treat us or let us down, His presence will always be with us. Even when we stray, He will go to the ends of the earth to bring us back into the fold. Nothing compares to being in the covenant family of the King of kings and Lord of lords. (Day 30)

PHASE FOUR
SEEKING TRUE GLORY

> But we all, with unveiled face, beholding as in a mirror the glory of the Lord, are being transformed into the same image from glory to glory, just as from the Lord, the Spirit. 2 Corinthians 3:18

Have you ever wondered why Christianity is illegal in so many countries? Deep in our hearts, we see the true God as either a gift or a threat. Jesus is either the source of our significance or a competitor for our individual crowns of glory and scepters of power. Ironically, what we sacrifice when we embrace Christ as Lord and Savior pales in comparison to what we gain. The martyred missionary Jim Elliot once wisely stated, "He is no fool who gives up what he cannot keep to gain what he cannot lose."

What we gain from being intimately connected with the King of kings and Lord of lords is almost beyond description. Looking upon our King's majestic goodness not only opens our eyes to our favored status, it also helps us realize how highly He has elevated us. This unearned combination of favor and status satisfies the root longings of the soul, heals the deepest hurts, and enables us to see through the fading facade of worldly glory. In the process, we are transformed as our thoughts, attitudes, words, and actions begin to align with heaven's glorious design.

The changes that God's glory produces within us are not only desirable, they are necessary. Owning a new identity in Christ often means becoming strangers, aliens, and outcasts in a place we call home. Furthermore, as Christians, we are identified (as Christ was) as enemies of our own culture. We will garner the courage to upset the status quo and stand strong for what we know to be true only as we become confident in our identities as royal children of the King.

DAY THIRTY-ONE
OUR HOPE OF GLORY

> God wanted to make known among the Gentiles the glorious wealth of this mystery, which is Christ in you, the hope of glory.
> Colossians 1:27 (HCSB)

When one thinks of the wondrous glory of Christ, how astonishing that He can join with us! But more, when one thinks of His bringing many sons to glory at such a cost, one is lost in adoring amazement.
—G. V. Wigram

If God's glory (i.e., His presence) served as the central identity of Israel, the departure of that presence (see Ezekiel 10 and 11) marked one of the most ignoble days of their entire history.

The nation persisted in its stubborn sin, spurning the Lord's repeated admonitions to abandon its idols. When it became evident that further patience was futile, God removed His glory from the temple that had been built by Solomon for the express purpose of housing His presence. Of all the priests and worshipers present, only the prophet Ezekiel noticed God's departure—the rest of the nation continued with business as usual. Then, in 587 BC, invading Babylonian armies destroyed the temple. In the process, the Ark of the Covenant—the very place where God's glory had dwelt—disappeared from human history.

After their seventy-year captivity in Babylon, returning exiles rebuilt the Israelite temple of worship, but it was not nearly as grand as the original. This second temple stood on Mount Moriah for five centuries, until the rise of King Herod the Great.

Herod decided to tear down that temple and rebuild it on a far grander scale. This building project lasted nearly ninety years. By the time Jesus arrived on the scene, the basic structure of what came to be called "Herod's temple" had been completed. Still, construction continued almost until the time when it was destroyed by Roman legions in 70 AD.

At the heart of the massive temple complex stood the main sanctuary—a seventeen-story structure built with brilliant white marble and adorned with glittering gold. The sanctuary was divided into two main parts—the *Holy Place* and the *Holy of Holies*. In this latter room, partitioned off by a thick veil of blue, purple, and scarlet cloth, the Jews honored God's presence as though He still resided there. Whether the glory of God was actually present is a matter of debate, for by and large, the room was empty. It held no Ark of the Covenant, no mercy seat, and no Ten Commandments. There was only a lone outcropping of rock; the Israelites believed that this was the stone upon which God had founded the world.

The overall design of the temple complex and its sanctuary communicated a poignant theme: *only a select few could draw near to God*. Anyone, including Gentiles (i.e., non-Jews) and corrupt sinners, could enter into the outer court. However, a short wall of three to four feet called the *Soreg* separated the outer court from the inner court, and only sanctified Jews could pass beyond it. Any Gentile who attempted to cross the *Soreg* would immediately be killed. Even Roman soldiers feared to raise the ire of their Jewish subjects.

Moving through a series of courtyards, openings, and stairs, the number of people allowed to enter shrank dramatically. Finally, only *one* person was permitted to go beyond the cloth veil and into the Holy of Holies. That individual was a male Jewish high priest who entered one day a year—on the Day of Atonement—to perform ceremonial duties. The message was clear: the closer you wanted to be to God's glory, the more spiritually elite you had to become. Thus, the temple stood as a symbol of stratification where only a few elite males had the privilege of drawing near to God.

Herod's temple was no doubt a grand, magnificent edifice, but God never meant for His presence to dwell in such an ornate structure (2 Samuel 7:1-7). In fact, Jesus scorned the thought of it (Mark 13:1-2). The sovereign King of Glory had a profoundly more majestic place in mind as an eternal dwelling to house His illustrious presence: *us*.

When Jesus died on the cross, the thick veil that separated the Holy of Holies from the rest of the sanctuary mysteriously tore in two from top to bottom. In a matter of seconds, there was no more separation, no more exclusivity. Through this supernatural event, God sent two powerful messages to humanity. First, His presence would never again be confined within the walls of an inanimate structure. Second, He would now give *all* people the opportunity for direct and unimpeded access to Himself. The tearing of the temple veil pointed toward God's incredible plan that broke all religious precedent: *people of all tribes and nations—including previously despised Gentiles—would become His new dwelling place.*

The idea of the living God dwelling within humanity is two-faceted. As individuals, each Christian is a "mini-temple" because that is where His presence dwells (1 Corinthians 6:19). Even more incredible, though, the Lord is building His people *together* into a "living temple"—a holy sanctuary of worshipers in whom He delights (1 Corinthians 3:10-16). With Jesus, glory became not only an individual concept but also a relational one.

> So then you are no longer strangers and aliens, but you are fellow citizens with the saints, and are of God's household, having been built on the foundation of the apostles and prophets, Christ Jesus Himself being the corner stone, in whom the whole building, being fitted together, is growing into a holy temple in the Lord, in whom you also are being built together into a dwelling of God in the Spirit.[1] Ephesians 2:19–22

It might seem impossible to construct a unified temple out of free-willed, diverse, and opinionated peoples, but the final result will be an edifice far more spectacular than anything ever constructed by human hands. This new temple will reveal a greater understanding of God's glory as His magnificence is expressed through a loving community of believers. God's glory and love cannot be confined by man-made structures; He lives within us.

---

1. The New Testament definition of a saint differs from common religious belief, which requires that sainthood be earned. The word saint means "holy one," referring to anyone who has been set apart from the corruption of this world for God's unique purposes. From a Biblical perspective, all genuine Christians are proclaimed to be saints.

Christ in us—this is our hope of glory. True significance comes from the presence of God dwelling within us, not from our ability to perform or from the approval and applause of others. This intimate association, we must remember, is a *gift of grace*; we cannot earn it. Any contradiction to this truth is but a tempting lie intended to ensnare us in sin and pride.

In Isaiah 42:8, the Lord stated that He would not give His "glory to another." But the context also tells us He will not share His glory with an idol, which is the objectification of a demon (Deuteronomy 32:16–17). Our heavenly Father despises idols, but He passionately desires to share His glory with His children. *The Almighty God ever seeks to house His glorious presence within human vessels and to build us into a spiritual sanctuary of living stones.* Simply amazing! I have no other words.

> The glory which You have given Me I have given to them, that they may be one, just as We are one; I in them and You in Me, that they may be perfected in unity, so that the world may know that You sent Me, and loved them, even as You have loved Me.
> John 17:22–23

QUESTIONS

1. What message did the design of the Jewish temple complex convey?

2. Please read Matthew 27:50–53. What is the significance of the veil of the temple being torn in two from top to bottom at the time of Christ's death?

3. If we have been clothed in eternal, divine glory, why are we consumed by the pursuit of human glory?

FURTHER READING: Matthew 27:45–54 and 1 Peter 2:4–5

PRAYER: I pray that the eyes of my heart may be enlightened, so I will know what is the hope of His calling, what are the riches of the glory of His inheritance in the saints, and what is the surpassing greatness of His power toward us who believe (Ephesians 1:18–19a).

DAY THIRTY-TWO
A ROYAL PRIESTHOOD

But you are not like that, for you are a chosen people. You are royal priests, a holy nation, God's very own possession. As a result, you can show others the goodness of God, for he called you out of the darkness into his wonderful light.
"Once you had no identity as a people;
    now you are God's people."

1 Peter 2:9–10a (NLT)

I have found that there are three stages in every great work of God: first, it is impossible, then it is difficult, then it is done.
—Hudson Taylor

"Do great things for God!" "Believe the impossible!" Both are messages I have heard during emotional "mountaintop" experiences when it seemed as though we could reach out and touch God. The high emotion of an inspirational meeting, however, differs vastly from the mundane grind of daily living.

It is in the spiritual valleys of our ordinary existence that we discover the impossible to be, well, impossible. A God-given vision, we must remember, will almost always contain an impossible element so that we learn to trust Him rather than our own prideful hearts. Thus, what once seemed like a glorious trek from a spiritual mountaintop can soon become a seemingly endless journey through the dark shadows of deep valleys.

In our efforts to fulfill a God-given vision, we often encounter a steady stream of frustrations and setbacks. That, at least, has been the case for me and countless others. When ministry feels as though it is going poorly, my inadequacies rise to the surface, and I am sorely tempted to rejoin the comparison game. While I sit in an obscure room staring at a computer screen, my social media feed delivers what seems to be a constant stream of success stories. All too often, I feel like an amateur in a world of professionals.

Ministry might not be your vocation, but if you have ventured out of your comfort zone in service to God, you can probably relate. Few are those who manage to stay perched on their spiritual mountaintops. The vast majority of us traverse plenty of dark valleys in our Christian journeys.

What should we do when the reality of our circumstances betrays the greatness of our vision? In those dark times, we must realize that we are a *royal priesthood* and that our *first* ministry is to the Lord.[1]

Old Testament priests played a unique and vital role. First, being a Jewish priest was an amazing privilege because those individuals alone had the honor of serving before the King of Glory. Everyone else stood at a distance, and non-Jews could not even get close.

> "You shall put the holy garments on Aaron and anoint him and consecrate him, that he may minister as a priest to Me. You shall bring his sons and put tunics on them; and you shall anoint them even as you have anointed their father, that they may minister as priests to Me; and their anointing will qualify them for a perpetual priesthood throughout their generations."
> Exodus 40:13–15

Moses' brother Aaron and his sons were "Levites," that is, descendants of Jacob's son Levi. As priests who ministered to God, they provided a physical representation of a greater spiritual reality to come. Specifically, I am referring to a prophecy given by Jeremiah:

> "As the host of heaven cannot be counted and the sand of the sea cannot be measured, so I will multiply the descendants of David My servant and the Levites who minister to Me."
> Jeremiah 33:22

What was the Lord saying through the prophet? One day, all His covenant children will form a royal priesthood that ministers to God

---

[1]. You might also consider reading my *Champions in the Wilderness* devotional!

and humanity. Peter's statement about Christians becoming royal priests marked the fulfillment of Jeremiah's prophecy.

How do we minister to God? With our *time*. We can spend time getting to know Him through His Word and also worshiping, praising, and giving thanks. Ministering to God with our time is how we cultivate an intimate relationship. There are no shortcuts.

In addition to ministering directly to the Almighty, Old Testament priests also served as go-betweens, mediators between man and God. Now, as His commissioned representatives, Christians bridge the gap between a holy Lord and all humanity. Praying for an unsaved neighbor, feeding the homeless, and even changing dirty diapers in the church nursery would all be considered priestly duties.

It is not the specific actions that mark our priestly ministry to humanity, but rather the motivations that flow from our relationship with the Lord. Under the old covenant, a priest had to perfectly follow the ritualistic requirements of the Mosaic law. Under the new covenant, however, ministry is no longer about perfect adherence to a set of laws. Jesus took care of that for us. Instead, serving God now centers around the basic motivation of *faith working through love* (see Galatians 5:6). The Lord wants us to trust Him in all that we do, and out of that trust flows a sacrificial love.

The Christian faith never revolves around religious perfection, but instead manifests itself through practical love. Of course, we want to set standards and pursue excellence in our work, but bringing pleasure to God has nothing to do with human measures of competency. *Being continually motivated by sincere faith and selfless love—that is where true glory lies.*

Would you like some advice that will spare you huge amounts of grief? Never forget that our first ministry is to God and our second is to humanity—in that necessary order. Keeping our priorities straight is vital for at least two reasons.

First, it is through our abiding relationship with the Lord that we are filled with the abundant life of the Holy Spirit. Ministering to others is to be the *overflow* of our relationship with our Lord. If we attempt to serve apart from His filling, we will quickly run dry, having nothing of significance left to give. Burnout is then but a few steps away.

A second reason we must make ministry to God our main priority is because those we serve will not always respond favorably. The apostle Paul was beaten (more than once), stoned, and imprisoned by the people he was trying to help. What makes us think we should be spared from such grief? If our ministry is to people first rather than God, indifference, criticism, betrayal, or even persecution on the part of those we are trying to bless might prove "fatal" to our ministry efforts. Under such circumstances, the likelihood of becoming hardened, cynical, and bitter rises exponentially.

Our efforts to help others will always have painful elements. People, after all, are basically enemies of God, but our heavenly reward will far outweigh any price we pay in service to the Lord.

> For God is not unjust so as to forget your work and the love which you have shown toward His name, in having ministered and in still ministering to the saints. Hebrews 6:10

No matter what mistakes we make, or how others respond to our efforts, our all-seeing Creator always knows the intentions of our hearts. When our ministry to humanity does not go as planned, we must remind ourselves that we are a royal priesthood and that our first ministry is to the Lord. We can hold fast to the assurance that our gracious Father sees all that we do for others in His name. *He will remember our sacrifices even when no one else seems to care.*

QUESTIONS

1. Why does God often call us to do things that are beyond our natural abilities?

2. What is the role of a priest?

3. Why is it vital that our *first* ministry be to the Lord?

FURTHER READING: 1 Peter 2:1–10 and Revelation 1:4–8

PRAYER: Lord, please help me to own my identity as a royal priest who serves You first and humanity second.

DAY THIRTY-THREE
THE BRIDE OF CHRIST

For I am jealous for you with the jealousy of God himself. I promised you as a pure bride to one husband—Christ.
2 Corinthians 11:2 (NLT)

Marriage is an adventure, like going to war.
—G. K. Chesterton

The cookie table—this tradition most likely started in Europe, but it is typical in eastern Ohio and western Pennsylvania where large numbers of European immigrants settled. Regardless of whether the wedding reception is being held in a fire hall (very common in small towns) or in an upscale venue, wedding guests are almost always treated to a table full of cookies when they enter the reception area.

The cookie selection is diverse. A guest might find chocolate chip, oatmeal raisin, cream horns, buckeyes, or snickerdoodles. An accompanying table might also have cheese and crackers, or possibly fresh fruit, but the appetizing spread of cookies is always present. The tasty treats help pass the time as the guests wait for the wedding party to have about four million pictures taken, but they certainly do not help keep waistlines slim.

Because we worked with college students for over sixteen years, Debi and I have been to more than our share of weddings. The variety has made for some interesting and unique experiences—such as the reception that was held at the Pittsburgh Zoo. There is nothing like snacking on a piece of homemade cheese with a shark peering over your shoulder.

When I make plans to officiate a wedding, I begin by giving a general outline to the bride and groom. Since it is "their day," they get to choose from among several optional elements, such as lighting a unity candle together. I also provide them with several ideas for the style of wording. Some couples prefer more traditional vows, while others choose to write their own.

There are some elements of a wedding ceremony that I consider to be non-negotiable, such as the exchanging of vows and rings, which are elements of a sacred covenant. A wedding is a *covenant ceremony* in which two individuals enter into a hallowed bond before God. No family is perfect, but a covenant relationship serves at least three primary functions.

First, a covenant is designed to create an environment in which intimacy thrives. Fidelity and security are two hallmarks of a thriving relationship. When trust is lost, meaningful intimacy vanishes.

Sexual intimacy often leads to the birth of children, which brings us to a second important purpose of the marriage covenant: creating a safe, healthy, and secure environment for raising children. When a husband and wife are devoted to one another in faithful love, their children have the best chance of growing into secure and healthy adults. This is not to say that all loving parents will raise well-adjusted children, or that a non-nuclear family spells certain disaster for a child. There are numerous variables involved with raising children, and so we find many trends but few guarantees.

The third—and greatest—purpose of the marriage covenant is to give us a tangible symbol of Christ's relationship with His church. The New Testament paints for us an image of Jesus as a *bridegroom* and the church as *His bride*. This relationship speaks of faithful love and intimacy but in a nonsexual way.

I will be honest with you; I purposely neglected to add "the bride of Christ" as an identity marker in my original outline for this book. It was not until a female friend in one of my studies questioned why the topic was missing that I made the change. I had no good answer other than to say that my masculine self struggles to relate to the idea of being a bride. The imagery, however, is profound.

Realizing that our human experiences often fall painfully short of the ideal, let us consider a few aspects of a marriage covenant that are relevant to our discussion about glory. Specifically, three vital earmarks of a healthy marriage are *intimate passion, sacrificial love,* and *faithful devotion.*

It might seem strange in our hyper-sexualized culture, but Debi and I did not sleep together before our wedding night. Even so, we counted down the days until we could enjoy unrestricted intimacy with one another. We burned with desire to be together, and marriage provided the fulfillment of that dream. Similarly, passion—nonsexual, but still intimate—is a huge driving factor for both Jesus and His bride, which is the church. In reality, He probably desires intimacy with us more than we do with Him—although the need is entirely ours. The book of Revelation tells us that heaven shares His excitement for that day to finally arrive:

> "Let us rejoice and be glad and give the glory to Him, for the marriage of the Lamb has come and His bride has made herself ready." Revelation 19:7

Jesus wants us. I mean, He *really* wants us! The angels of heaven are all aware of this reality as they make preparations for a great feast to celebrate this union (see Matthew 22:1–14 for more imagery). Just as Debi and I counted down the days until our wedding, all of heaven eagerly anticipates the marriage of the Lamb.

Another key element of a marriage covenant is *sacrificial love*. Much has already been said about the huge sacrifices Jesus made on our behalf. In a passage of Scripture commonly read at weddings, Paul made the connection between Christ's sacrificial love and the marriage covenant:

> Husbands, love your wives, just as Christ also loved the church and gave Himself up for her, so that He might sanctify her, having cleansed her by the washing of water with the word, that He might present to Himself the church in all her glory, having no spot or wrinkle or any such thing; but that she would be holy and blameless. Ephesians 5:25–27

The third element of a healthy marriage is *faithful devotion*. In many Middle Eastern cultures, this unwavering devotion begins with the couple's engagement (betrothal). For all intents and purposes, the two are considered to be married the day they get engaged. They do not, however, sexually consummate their relationship until the day of the wedding, which might be about a year later. This was the case with Mary and Joseph—they were "betrothed" when she (though still a virgin) was found to be with child by the Holy Spirit.

I tend to view *water baptism* as a kind of betrothal ceremony. Through water baptism, a person makes a public declaration that he or she will be faithfully devoted to the Lord forever. Between now and when we are joined with Jesus in heaven, Christians in this world pursue Him as their "First Love." This means having no other gods before Him, whatever form they might happen to take.

Intimate passion, sacrificial love, and faithful devotion—all are integral elements of a healthy marriage, and all reflect Jesus' heart toward us. A key aspect of a bride's glory is that her groom wants her so much that he is willing to forsake all other loves to have her as his wife. Has not Jesus, through His actions, similarly demonstrated an intense desire for us? But unlike some spouses, His faithfulness never ends.

How much time and energy do you spend trying to undo deep-seated feelings of shame—to prove that you are worthy of significance and honor? Do you realize you are the focus of Christ's passion? Can you grasp the intense, emotion-filled love that Jesus has for you? The King of Glory wants *you* with all of His heart! Now, that is something to get excited about!

QUESTIONS

1. Read Ephesians 5:22–32. How is marriage intended to help us understand the relationship between Christ and His church?

2. In what way is water baptism like a betrothal ceremony?

3. How does it make you feel to know that Jesus passionately desires to be with you?

FURTHER READING: Isaiah 62:1–5 and Revelation 19:7–9

PRAYER: Jesus, may my passion for You be as strong and as vibrant as Your passion for me.

DAY THIRTY-FOUR
KINGDOM AMBASSADORS

For He rescued us from the domain of darkness, and transferred us to the kingdom of His beloved Son, in whom we have redemption, the forgiveness of sins.

Colossians 1:13–14

If a commission by an earthly king is considered an honor, how can a commission by a Heavenly King be considered a sacrifice?
—David Livingstone

Born and living in Hungary, seventeen-year-old Elizabeth met a young man who promised her a better life. She responded quickly to his almost-immediate marriage proposal, but there was a problem. Michael worked as a coal miner in the United States, and he was unable to take her on his return trip. She would have to wait until he earned enough money to pay for her travel.

Elizabeth waited, and Michael held true to his word. Soon, she embarked upon the long journey to Ellis Island in New York Harbor. Once again, a lack of money hindered their plans. The funds Michael saved were only enough to get her to New York; she had nothing left for the train ticket to his home in western Pennsylvania. This young Hungarian woman, unable to speak English, and a stranger to a new country, waited courageously on Ellis Island for over a week until the much-needed provision for her journey came through.

One of Elizabeth's proudest moments was when she passed her citizenship test. My grandmother felt incredibly special—a full-fledged citizen of what many called "the greatest country in the world." Nagymama (i.e., "grandmother" in Hungarian) never lost her love for her native Hungary, but oh how she cherished the opportunity to become a citizen of a nation founded on freedom, opportunity, and promise!

The Bible speaks of a higher citizenship; the *kingdom of God* is a realm dwarfing even the greatest on earth. This government, unlike the flawed examples with which we are familiar, is perfect in every way. Never has there been a monarch like the King of Glory; He rules by an astute love and metes out justice without partiality. There are no strangers or outsiders in God's kingdom, only fellow citizens with the saints.

The kingdom of God is also one of *equality*. While the kingdoms of humanity function by *stratification*—the elite rising above the commoners—His government is characterized by *edification*. The citizens of God's kingdom do not pridefully lift themselves above others, but humbly seek the success and well-being of all.

Human kingdoms are governed by massive volumes of law, restricting freedom and placing heavy burdens on the shoulders of their citizens. In contrast, Christ's kingdom is ruled by the *law of liberty* (James 1:25) through which the freedom to choose is motivated by virtuous love.

Earthly governments are often beset by conflict, relying on guns and prisons to keep antagonists from further destroying the peace. In contrast, the kingdom of God is one of unity and peace without conflict. There is no division in God's kingdom because when there are no glory deficiencies, the sources of animosity that divide us vaporize into thin air.

The unity of God's kingdom provides an amazing reflection of His glory—more glorious than the hundreds of billions of stars that make up the hundreds of billions of galaxies in our universe. Diverse peoples of every race, tribe, and tongue willingly come together as one. Judgmental attitudes, discord, shame, exploitation, oppression, and injustice are entirely absent from the King's realm.

Although this description might sound like a far-off ideal, God intends His kingdom on earth to be an extension of His realm in heaven. We will experience its fullness on a day yet to come, but the kingdom is here now and is expanding to fill the earth. *All other nations will eventually crumble into rubble and dust, but God's good government is guaranteed to rule forever.*

Much of the chaos we see in our world today is due to a "shaking" process in which true, substantive glory is being separated from pseudo-glory. No doubt, there are times when steady streams of bad news make us feel as though this world is spinning out of control, but a brilliant plan is being accomplished nonetheless. The King of Glory still reigns, and He continues to work powerfully as people invite Him into their lives, families, and circumstances.

Natural disasters, wars, and government upheavals are tragic in many ways, but they also present vital opportunities for our Lord to rescue lost souls from an eternity apart from His presence. It is here that the current citizens of God's realm play an invaluable role. Citizenship in His kingdom is *voluntary*. It comes not through the involuntary process of natural birth, but through the opportunity to embrace Christ as Lord and Savior. Because participation is not compulsory, and because God's kingdom is invisible to the natural eye, His citizens serve as *ambassadors* who proclaim His goodness and display His glory. The apostle Paul described the privilege of becoming ambassadors for Christ:

> Now all these things are from God, who reconciled us to Himself through Christ and gave us the ministry of reconciliation, namely, that God was in Christ reconciling the world to Himself, not counting their trespasses against them, and He has committed to us the word of reconciliation.
>
> Therefore, we are ambassadors for Christ, as though God were making an appeal through us; we beg you on behalf of Christ, be reconciled to God. 2 Corinthians 5:18–20

Being designated as an ambassador for Christ's heavenly realm is an amazing honor. But it also requires a new mindset that breaks from past thought patterns. To represent Him well we must:

1. Learn the dynamics of being a citizen of the kingdom of God. This is both for our benefit and that we might fully understand who and what we represent.

2. Give the highest priority to the ministry of reconciliation to which He has called us. Indeed, our ambassadorship is a primary reason we continue to live on earthly soil.

We have already seen that it is not enough to simply do ministry and build churches in the name of God since we are predisposed to grand visions for personal glory. God's kingdom does not work in this way, and ego-driven efforts will eventually crash. Our ambassadorship is for *His* kingdom and His kingdom alone.

3. Treat our influence with others (i.e., our Christian witness) as though it is one of our most prized "possessions." We have an amazing opportunity to invite others to become citizens of the kingdom of light. But if our lifestyles are incongruent with our profession of faith, kingdom influence will be squandered.

Being an ambassador for Christ presents both an honor and an opportunity. We do not need to be perfect Christians to fulfill this call; we need only to be willing to grow in His love and grace. If the ministry of reconciliation was important enough for Jesus to descend from heaven and sacrificially give His life, it is important enough for us to make it central to our short stay on this planet. *Truly glorious living involves not just receiving the benefits of what God has done for us, but also helping to reconcile others to a meaningful relationship with our amazing King of Glory.*

QUESTIONS

1. Why does our citizenship in God's kingdom dwarf that of any earthly nation?

2. Name some ways that the kingdom of God differs from the governments that populate our planet.

3. What makes our Christian witness so amazingly valuable?

FURTHER READING: Daniel 2:1–45 and Acts 1:1–8

PRAYER: King Jesus, please give me grace to live a life that accurately reflects my citizenship in Your kingdom, and instill within me the passion and ability needed to be an effective ambassador for You.

DAY THIRTY-FIVE
JOINT HEIRS WITH CHRIST

The Spirit Himself testifies with our spirit that we are children of God, and if children, heirs also, heirs of God and fellow heirs with Christ, if indeed we suffer with Him so that we may also be glorified with Him.

Romans 8:16–17

Why would we want fame, when God promises us glory? Why would we be seeking the wealth of the world when the wealth of heaven is ours? Why would we run for a crown that will perish with time, when we're called to win a crown that is imperishable?
—Paul David Washer

Claudia Moretti inherited a home in Italy from her late uncle. In the house was a safe containing 100 million lire—about $70,000 U.S. dollars. Thinking she had struck it rich, Ms. Moretti went to a bank to exchange the cash for euros. Only then did she learn of a huge problem. Upon adopting the euro in 2002, Italian officials had declared that their own currency would be nullified after December 6, 2011. Claudia's 100 million lire inheritance was now worthless.[1]

In another case, a woman inherited a family heirloom from her late husband that everyone thought was worthless. Experts then appraised the painting at over $1,300,000. She claimed that family members suddenly cared a great deal about the heirloom.[2]

These stories remind me of the difference between a temporary human inheritance with no lasting value, and an eternal one from

---

1. "Sorry, your 100 million lire is worthless: bank," *The Local.it*, March 12, 2014, accessed April 02, 2024, https://www.thelocal.it/20140312/italians-100-million-lira-worth-nothing.
2. Laura Suter, "Moral Money: My late husband's 'worthless' family heirloom is actually worth £1m. Who owns it, me or his family?", The Telegraph, July 5, 2017, accessed April 02, 2024, http://www.telegraph.co.uk/money/consumer-affairs/moral-money-late-husbands-worthless-family-heirloom-actually/.

God which often goes ignored. This contrast between a temporary and lasting inheritance is also evident in the Bible. In the Old Testament, the Lord promised Abraham that his descendants would inherit the land of Canaan (Genesis 13:12-17). In the New Testament, God promises that His covenant children will inherit His unseen kingdom. The emphasis transitions from physical to spiritual.

Being spiritual in nature, a new covenant inheritance is also *eternal*. I cannot help thinking that *spiritual* also means *mysterious* because I find myself challenged to envision how such an inheritance will look. I am not alone in my struggle. The apostle Paul prayed for the Ephesian church that "the eyes of their hearts would be enlightened" that they might know "what are the riches of the glory of His inheritance in the saints" (Ephesians 1:18).

Paul's letter to the Romans tells us that we are "fellow heirs with Christ" (Romans 8:16-17). It seems that the inheritance is Christ's, and that as God's covenant children, we all receive our share. The situation is a little strange, though, because the bulk of our inheritance will be received only *after* our bodies are laid to rest.[3]

As members of God's family, we will inherit the royal kingdom. Consider what Jesus' half-brother James tells us:

> Listen, my beloved brethren: did not God choose the poor of this world to be rich in faith and heirs of the kingdom which He promised to those who love Him? James 2:5

Once again, we find a stark contrast between natural and spiritual mindsets. Earthly kings tend to consolidate power by killing off potential threats to their thrones, but the King of Glory has taken the opposite approach. Even though we were once enemies who joined a rebellion against the throne of heaven, He still destines us to share the wealth of His kingdom. After all, giving us the kingdom of God as our inheritance was *His* idea (see Luke 12:32).

What do we know about the kingdom of God? It is a realm of power and authority that reigns over all dark forces. The kingdom is

---

3. Strange as it might seem, Jesus never treated death as a permanent state. In fact, He often confused people by equating death with *falling asleep* (see John 11:11-14). Christ's perspective presupposes that what we call "death" is merely a transition, and that all Christians will one day be raised to a new and eternal life.

characterized by righteousness, peace, and joy (Romans 14:17). And though we do not know much about the full extent of our kingdom inheritance, thanks to Peter, we know something about its enduring quality.

> Blessed be the God and Father of our Lord Jesus Christ, who according to His great mercy has caused us to be born again to a living hope through the resurrection of Jesus Christ from the dead, to obtain an inheritance which is imperishable and undefiled and will not fade away, reserved in heaven for you, who are protected by the power of God through faith for a salvation ready to be revealed in the last time. 1 Peter 1:3–5

"Imperishable." "Undefiled." "Will not fade away." These ideas echo what Jesus said about storing up eternal treasures in heaven:

> "Do not store up for yourselves treasures on earth, where moth and rust destroy, and where thieves break in and steal. But store up for yourselves treasures in heaven, where neither moth nor rust destroys, and where thieves do not break in or steal; for where your treasure is, there your heart will be also." Matthew 6:19–21

Peter also tells his readers that they were not "redeemed with perishable things like silver or gold" from the "futile way of life" inherited from their forefathers (1 Peter 1:18). Such statements cause me to stop and think about what I value.

The contrast between an earthly and heavenly inheritance is clear. The former is subject to natural forces such as theft and devaluation, while the latter endures forever. In terms of value and desirability, the two cannot even be compared.

The Bible also tells us that God has already given us a down payment on our eternal inheritance: *the Holy Spirit!*

> In Him, you also, after listening to the message of truth, the gospel of your salvation—having also believed, you were sealed in Him with the Holy Spirit of promise, who is given

as a pledge of our inheritance, with a view to the redemption of God's own possession, to the praise of His glory. Ephesians 1:13–14

This passage is incredible! *The pledge of our eternal inheritance is the presence of God Himself.* Why would we want anything more?

The resurrection of Jesus makes our glorious inheritance possible. Through the power of Christ's blood, we become spotless vessels in which His Spirit dwells. And through His eternal life, we are resurrected into a new destiny. Thus, God gives us a taste of our inheritance now through His Spirit, and we will receive the remainder in the next life.

Considering the amazing value of an eternal inheritance in Christ, we are again reminded of human shortsightedness. Untold numbers of people approach Christian involvement with a yawn of indifference. It is like the heirloom that the woman inherited from her husband; nobody cared until an expert appraised the painting.

The "day of appraisal" will come when those with worldly mindsets find themselves holding rotted, rusted, and corrupted "treasures." On that day, everyone will pine for a share of God's inheritance. Please do not make the mistake of putting your hope in perishable treasures that rust and fade away. Draw near to the Lord *now*, and embrace the glorious gift of the Holy Spirit which He yearns to give to you!

QUESTIONS

1. What are some of the differences between a natural inheritance and our spiritual inheritance in Christ?

2. What are some of the ramifications of the Holy Spirit being a "down payment" for our eternal inheritance?

3. How do you think people will respond on "the day of appraisal"?

FURTHER READING: Romans 8:15–25 and 1 Peter 1:13–25

PRAYER: Heavenly Father, please fill me with your eternal Spirit!

DAY THIRTY-SIX
SEATED IN HEAVENLY PLACES

But God, being rich in mercy, because of His great love with which He loved us, even when we were dead in our transgressions, made us alive together with Christ (by grace you have been saved), and raised us up with Him, and seated us with Him in the heavenly places in Christ Jesus, so that in the ages to come He might show the surpassing riches of His grace in kindness toward us in Christ Jesus.

Ephesians 2:4–7

On the head of Christ are many crowns. He wears the crown of victory; he wears the crown of sovereignty; he wears the crown of creation; he wears the crown of providence; he wears the crown of grace; he wears the crown of glory—for every one of his glorified people owes his honor, happiness and blessedness to him.
—James H. Aughey

I have shared the story before, but it never gets old. One day, after he had consolidated his throne, King David began thinking of times gone by, of old friendships, and especially of his covenant with his deceased friend Jonathan. "Is there yet anyone left of the house of Saul, that I may show him my kindness for Jonathan's sake?" David inquired of those around him (2 Samuel 9:1).

The fact that David would ask such a question for benevolent purposes is quite strange. Ancient kings were known to seek out and execute potential competitors to their thrones. History is awash with stories of monarchs (e.g., King Herod) who killed even their own children in ruthless efforts to keep and consolidate power.

David's inquiry led to the discovery that one of Jonathan's sons was indeed still alive, but Mephibosheth's story was a sad one. His grandfather Saul (the former king) and his father Jonathan had been slain in battle by the Philistines during a tragic defeat for Israel. Moreover, while attempting to carry him to safety, Mephibosheth's nurse accidentally dropped the then five-year-old, seriously injuring both of his feet. Mephibosheth was now lame.

Names carry considerable meaning in Jewish culture, and it is interesting to note that Mephibosheth was also known at times as "Meribaal"—a moniker fit for a king, with *baal* meaning "lord." The linguistics are not clear, but it is likely that the young man was initially given a noble name meaning "from the mouth of the lord," only to have it changed to one meaning "from the mouth of shame."[1]

According to cultural standards, Jonathan's son had been thoroughly disgraced. God had removed his family from the throne and replaced it with a new lineage, his father and grandfather had been slain in a losing battle, and he had been crippled in both feet. In a masculine, warring culture, Mephibosheth was indeed "out of the mouth of shame."

Falling on his face before the king, Mephibosheth understood well the precariousness of his position. All he had to offer King David was potential competition for his throne. Even if Saul's grandson could not wield a sword and command an army, there was still the possibility that his descendants would threaten David's own royal lineage.

Recognizing the young man's anxiousness, David calmed his fears with words that were as surprising as they were reassuring:

> "Do not fear, for I will surely show kindness to you for the sake of your father Jonathan, and will restore to you all the land of your grandfather Saul; and you shall eat at my table regularly."
> 2 Samuel 9:7

Mephibosheth's change of fortunes was extreme. Having plummeted from a life of promise into shame and obscurity, he came trembling at the king's call. Now, he was being lifted again to a place of honor and invited to dine regularly with the king's sons, other nobles, and visiting dignitaries. Furthermore, Mephibosheth would no longer

---

1. *Who's Who in the Bible* (Pleasantville, NY: The Readers Digest Association, Inc., 1994), 293.

have to depend upon the provision of others, as David also made him the master of a large property.

Why did this situation transpire? It was not because of any greatness within Mephibosheth, but because of David's covenant with his father. How did Mephibosheth respond? "What is your servant, that you should regard a dead dog like me?" (2 Samuel 9:8).

I cannot help but think that the apostle Paul had this story in mind when he penned his letter to the Ephesians. In a very real sense, Paul was saying that we were "dead-dog" sinners worthy only of shame and disgrace. But because of God's rich mercy, He sent Jesus to suffer and die for our sins. That single act of humble, faithful love has lifted us from the dregs of infamy to a seat of amazing honor.

The significance of being "seated with Christ in heavenly places" is beyond profound considering His exalted status:

> These are in accordance with the working of the strength of His might which He brought about in Christ, when He raised Him from the dead and seated Him at His right hand in the heavenly places, far above all rule and authority and power and dominion, and every name that is named, not only in this age but also in the one to come. Ephesians 1:19b–21

The King of Glory reigns over *everything*, and nothing anyone thinks, says, or does will ever change that. He is the sovereign Lord of the universe, and whatever He decrees becomes the law of the land.

What are the ramifications for us? Christians are not just being lifted up to be saved, but also to be honored. This is—and always has been—our Creator's intention for the human race. *God wants to cover and clothe us in His glory, every bit as much as we need to have our glory deficiencies satisfied.*

As amazing as these ideas sound, their reality is actually more incredible than we realize because being seated with Christ in heavenly places is also a matter of *authority*. By His grace, the Almighty gives His covenant children the authority to "tread on serpents and scorpions and over all the power of the enemy" (Luke 10:19). This, too, is the fulfillment of God's plan which He initiated in the garden of Eden when He gave humans dominion over the earth.

When we abide in His grace, we have far more power and authority than often realized.

To fully enjoy this privileged status (and to exercise our God-given authority), we must remember *why* we are given this honor. It is never because of our own merits—we were all dead-dog sinners—but it is due to the covenant which Jesus, the Son of Man, established with the heavenly Father on our behalf. Glory and authority are *gifts* from God; we cannot reach out and grab them for ourselves.

The Pharisees tried to position themselves in seats of glory and power and were rejected by God as a result (Luke 11:43). Foolishly, they abandoned unfading glory for the sake of fig-leaf images and human approval. These men forfeited any eternal inheritance from the God they professed to serve, instead opting for fleeting moments of human affirmation as their *full* reward (Matthew 6:1–6).

The Pharisees failed to understand that we can receive glory as an unearned gift, but we cannot take it for ourselves. The Lord lifts us up when we choose to live humbly. But when we selfishly grab for honor, true, substantive glory eludes our grasp.

The Lord has delivered us—former dead-dog sinners and enemies of His throne—from the mouth of shame, and He has seated us with Him in heavenly places of glory, honor, and authority. How else can we respond but with humble gratitude and words of praise?

QUESTIONS

1. What were some of the shameful elements of Mephibosheth's life?

2. What was King David's primary reason for giving Mephibosheth a place of honor at the king's table, and how does this correlate with Ephesians 2:1–10?

3. Please explain what it means to say, "We can receive glory as an unearned gift, but we cannot take it for ourselves."

FURTHER READING: 2 Samuel 9 and Ephesians 1:15–2:10

PRAYER: Lord, there is no comparison between what I deserve and how You have honored me. Thank you so much!

DAY THIRTY-SEVEN
GLORY OUT OF WEAKNESS

And He has said to me, "My grace is sufficient for you, for power is perfected in weakness." Most gladly, therefore, I will rather boast about my weaknesses, so that the power of Christ may dwell in me. Therefore I am well content with weaknesses, with insults, with distresses, with persecutions, with difficulties, for Christ's sake; for when I am weak, then I am strong.
2 Corinthians 12:9–10

Grace is but glory begun, and glory is but grace perfected.
—Jonathan Edwards

I am a strong advocate of the Bible, not because I like everything it says, but because I know it to be true. I have also realized that many of our cultural mindsets are rooted in lies, including our perspectives of strength and weakness. In this world, personal strength establishes the foundation for success, and weakness is considered a liability. We boast of strength, weakness not so much. In the dynamics of God's kingdom, however, strength is often a liability, while weakness forms the building blocks from which spiritual prosperity flows. Personal experiences, however, often speak otherwise.

Many of us are terrified to reveal our weaknesses because of the potential for humiliation. Remember the fear and shame that Adam and Eve felt after eating the forbidden fruit? Humans are not so gracious as God was in Eden, and so public displays of weakness serve as open invitations for ridicule and oppression.

We often face ridicule when we fail to meet societal expectations because of weakness, appearance, or an inability to conform to social norms. Therefore, to avoid the pain of culture-induced shame, we labor nonstop to hide our weaknesses, to measure up to standards, and to portray fig-leaf images of "having it all together." The problem with our "pretend everything is great" approach, however, is that it opposes the dynamics of God's empowering grace.

The apostle Paul's "celebration of weakness" in 2 Corinthians 12:9–10 would be considered outlandish for any culture. What red-blooded male chooses to boast about his weaknesses? Have you ever seen a young boy brag about his inability? Of course not. Humanity idolizes strength and despises weakness, but it is through the latter that God's glory shines.

The Bible says the whole earth will one day be filled with the glory of the Lord (Numbers 14:21). The full expression of this brilliant reality will be revealed only after every "mountain" is brought low, and every "valley" is raised up (Isaiah 40:4). Isaiah's figurative language refers to the state of human hearts. *The age of grace, which we are in, is characterized by bringing down the arrogant and lifting up the humble in preparation for Christ's return.* This is awesome news for some people but nothing short of dreadful for others.

Regardless of where we individually sit on the pride-humility continuum, grand adventures with God are never devoid of weakness and the pain that frequently accompanies it. Humans will always seek to exalt themselves, but our wise King allows no flesh to glory in His presence (1 Corinthians 1:29). Thus, He uses the shortcomings that we think disqualify us from effective ministry to establish a foundation of humility to better prepare us for fruitful service.

How odd, if not offensive, is the gospel of grace in a world bent on displaying its strength. Christ, our Savior and our example, calls us to let go of facade-like images to embrace the substance of true glory. This can appear to be an undesirable road and is likely why so few men seem to populate many Christian circles.

Many males view Bible-based Christianity as a dangerous minefield of potential humiliation. In the rural areas where I have always lived, men have traditionally avoided reading (the Bible included), preferring instead to play sports, enjoy the outdoors, and work with their hands. They have also tended to view prayer and worship as feminine activities. Furthermore, asking questions about spiritual principles can be embarrassing in that it reveals a potential ignorance—yet another expression of weakness. And most significantly, being a fully devoted follower of Christ requires the type of humility that puts our masculine pride at risk, making us vulnerable to the shame of public ridicule.

I am not suggesting that we broadcast our struggles and shortcomings to the world; there are plenty of uncaring people who will respond with callous cruelty. But we do need to find loving, supportive, and trustworthy people with whom we can bare the depths of our souls in times of need—times which we all have. When we do this, even our most painful journeys can lay the groundwork for future glory. Much to my chagrin, the most powerful breakthroughs in my life have come after humbling myself and owning my weakness by asking for help.

The pursuit of fleeting human glory keeps us enslaved, but the true substance of divine glory sets our hearts free. However, we must let go of pretentious images if we want to lay hold of glory's true substance. The core of our struggle lies here: *our pride must die for God's glory to be fully realized in our lives.*

One of the keys to humility—and thus glory—involves "owning" our human weakness. How we wish this Biblical truth were a falsehood! Until we can be honest and accept our weaknesses, we will be starved of the grace needed to defeat our demons.

The benefit of finding empowering grace through weakness is a primary reason the Bible treats *fasting* as a normal practice. By voluntarily abstaining from food, followers of God receive a powerful reminder of their own fragility, and thus, of their humbling dependence upon the Lord's life-giving sustenance.

As long as we are in this world, the temptation to find glory in ourselves, independent from our Creator, will never abate. And the nearer we draw to the King of Glory, the more intensely the powers of darkness will work to pull us back into their deadly grip. We must take deliberate and practical steps to draw upon God's strength.

Imperfect human flesh has no logical reason for boasting, but boast it does. Therefore, it is no coincidence that Jesus told His disciples to carry their crosses daily (Luke 9:23). Perhaps He chose the slow, painful death of crucifixion as His own method of sacrifice to reinforce this message. Furthermore, both His resurrection and ascension to heaven provide hope-filled images for our future destiny. When our time here reaches its finality, these frail bodies, having been sown in weakness into earthen soil, will be raised and transformed into the glorious likeness of Christ's resurrected body.

Can you see the Lord's ingenious plan at work? He does not want to leave anyone out in the cold, and yet only gives glory to His royal children. Why? Only they have been given the new hearts that can handle glory's euphoria without becoming corrupted by pride.

Times of weakness, struggle, and adversity are not indicators of God's abandonment, but rather *opportunities* for us to put off the old and put on the new. We face a grave danger in our time to become hardened, cynical, and unbelieving in response to the attitudes and actions of a cruel, unjust world. But as the covenant children of God, we live differently, encouraging and strengthening one another to persevere through trial and tribulation.

If you are anything like me, you have had more than your share of struggles in life. It makes no difference who is to blame for our present difficulties. *As His royal children, we can rest assured that He lovingly and diligently uses all of our sufferings to prepare us for future glory.* Be encouraged; that day will surely come and render our current pain a distant memory.

Both God and the devil are ever at work, but if we choose to walk humbly together, our "momentary light affliction" will produce "an eternal weight of glory far beyond all comparison" (2 Corinthians 4:17). At the end of this earthly road, what was once our weak and undesirable journey will make us the envy of the entire world.

QUESTIONS

1. Why do we despise weakness so much?

2. Why is weakness necessary for grace to have its full effect in our lives?

3. How do current difficulties help prepare us for future glory?

FURTHER READING: 1 Corinthians 15:42–58 and 2 Corinthians 4

PRAYER: Lord, please grant me the wisdom and grace to exchange my weakness for Your strength.

DAY THIRTY-EIGHT
THE HIGH ROAD OF HUMILITY

"For I know the plans that I have for you," declares the Lord, "plans for welfare and not for calamity to give you a future and a hope."

Jeremiah 29:11

The labor of self-love is a heavy one indeed. Think whether much of your sorrow has not arisen from someone speaking slightingly of you. As long as you set yourself up as a little god to which you must be loyal, there will be those who delight to offer affront to your idol.

—A. W. Tozer

No single stereotype can be applied to our local university students; they come in an array of shapes, sizes, and colors, with all manner of dress. But some appearances simply do not blend, and that was the case one morning as I drove past the school on the way to my office.

A slightly overweight, middle-aged white guy wearing a dark suit and matching tie captured my eye (no, I was not looking in the mirror). There he stood on a busy sidewalk, holding a stack of small Bibles in one hand, and trying to give them to students with the other. The disinterest was obvious. Not one person made eye contact with the man during the time I sat and waited for the traffic light to turn green.

Getting a college degree is a costly endeavor; it requires tens of thousands of dollars, several years of study, and considerable dedication. Millions of people choose a college path because they are told by the authorities in their lives that at the end of the trail shines the promise of a meaningful and profitable career. Such a career is vital not only for provision, but also for significance. In this performance-driven world, our work naturally becomes our identity.

I have no qualms about pursuing a college education—my own life has been greatly enriched by the experience—but the image of young people scurrying for success and significance while ignoring the Word of God leaves me at a loss. When I worked in college ministry, I sometimes led orientation sessions for parents who were inquiring about religious groups on campus. A typical session averaged about six to eight people, while the career-related meetings overflowed with parents doing all they could to help their children succeed in the material realm.

During my sixteen years on campus, I found many of the students to be emotionally broken. Whether their pain was tied to a dysfunctional family, neighborhood bullying, or fear of an uncertain tomorrow, intellectual prowess did nothing to heal their wounds and calm their fears. Even as they succeeded in the various facets of college life, their pain and fear continued to linger, waiting to strike like a shark cruising beneath the surface of the water.

Just like the rest of society, our universities are filled with broken people. Every individual needs a revelation of God and His goodness, but the messages preached in career settings make no mention of the King of Glory. "Work hard! Apply yourself! Network with successful people. Do these things, and you will find true significance as you climb the ladder of success." Dedication and hard work are undoubtedly vital assets, but worldly success fails miserably as a means of satisfying our inherent glory deficiencies.

Pursuing earthly glory, we construct lofty—and unattainable— images of our "perfect" selves. Thus, we seek to be stellar parents, flawless athletes, and highly productive workers. The problem, however, lies not with our goals but with our *motives*.

Many of us drain our life's energy fleeing from shame-inducing circumstances, ignoble failures, and embarrassing shortcomings, somehow believing that the glory of success will eradicate our Ichabod pasts. It will not. Untold numbers of dedicated people have climbed the ladder of success, only to find themselves as empty at the top as they were at the bottom. Worse still, when they fail to find fulfillment, a deep-seated sense of disappointment takes root because the pursuit of significance through success is the only path to self-worth they have ever known.

Many psychologists and even pastors say we need to learn how to love ourselves, but the truth is that we all love ourselves. Self-love is why we labor to meet our needs first, why we want to jump to the head of the line, and why we hide tasty food in the back of the refrigerator so no one else will eat it. Ironically, self-love is also why we become codependent enablers, neglecting our own needs while serving "selflessly" to "save" another person. Feeling needed makes us feel significant. Human nature can be so confusing!

What we call "self-hatred" is actually a twisted form of self-love that despises our personal shortcomings, and which, more often than not, is imposed upon us by the opinions of others. I might look at my blemished face in the mirror and exclaim, "I hate myself!" But what I really mean is that I love myself so much that I cannot accept the negative opinion others have imposed upon me.

God will wisely allow certain "inglorious" elements in our lives—dysfunctional family, short stature, and lack of athletic ability as examples—so that we might not find glory in ourselves, but look to Him for significance and purpose. Coming to peace with the unchangeable things we despise will have a powerful effect on both our emotional well-being and our future destiny. (I do not consider an abusive situation to be unchangeable. If you are being abused by anyone, including a family member, please seek help.)

We live in a fallen world, but the Lord promises to turn *every* negative toward the fulfillment of His good purposes (Romans 8:28). Thinking that God loves you less is tantamount to calling Him a liar, and that will get you nowhere good. Again, the secret lies in learning to *accept* the unchangeable negatives in your life. Not only do these things provide powerful platforms for humility and grace, the Lord will also interweave them with a desirable destiny.

I now accept many things about my life that I once hated, realizing that if I had gotten what I wanted, my ego would have blossomed into arrogance. Furthermore, the moment I accepted what He had allowed, the path to my God-given destiny began to emerge. If not for the undesirable elements of my past, I would not be blessed to influence others in the way that I am.

The gospel provides a profound opportunity for people who are nobodies in the eyes of the world to become somebodies, but all too often, we attempt to apply our human methods of finding significance to our Christian experience. This never works. What we do not realize is that our failures and shortcomings help establish a foundation of humility that enables us to do great things without the euphoria of success inflating our egos.

One of the greatest mysteries of life revolves around the fact that true greatness is found on the "high road of humility." The road is high because those who travel its course capture our Creator's attention, but it is also low because it often makes us appear inglorious in the eyes of the world. Few of us seem willing to embrace the truth that God does some of His most magnificent work in and through broken, inadequate people who lack the markers of worldly glory.

The Lord calls us to discover His awe-inspiring design for our lives and to align ourselves accordingly. God will not do these things for us. Those who seek true and lasting significance must stop fretting about their negative circumstances and attributes. Fretting over an imperfect life will make it less ideal, and fixating on our shortcomings will further stall the fulfillment of God's good plans.

The all-wise Creator knows what He is doing. He longs to lift us up and use us in significant ways, but this process depends on our willingness to align ourselves with His design by learning to trust Him in the face of negative circumstances. The path to our God-given destinies follows the high road of humility, and we must learn to accept His mysteries along the way.

QUESTIONS

1. What value can the negative aspects of our lives bring to us?

2. What is the difference between self-acceptance and self-love?

3. Why is it self-defeating to fret about undesirable circumstances?

FURTHER READING: Psalm 138 and 1 Corinthians 1:26–31

PRAYER: God, grant me the serenity to accept the things I cannot change; courage to change the things I can; and wisdom to know the difference. (Serenity Prayer by Reinhold Niebuhr)

DAY THIRTY-NINE
HIDDEN GLORY

For I consider that the sufferings of this present time are not worthy to be compared with the glory that is to be revealed to us. For the anxious longing of the creation waits eagerly for the revealing of the sons of God.

Romans 8:18–19

Endurance is not just the ability to bear a hard thing, but to turn it into glory.

—William Barclay

Through the course of reading this devotional you have probably had more than a few questions about your own spiritual condition, and about whether you are beset by a glory deficiency. The following simple test will help answer that question.

Take the palm of your dominant hand and rest it on the back of your other hand. Do you feel any measure of warmth? Then take your index and middle fingers from your dominant hand and place them on your opposite wrist to check your pulse. Do you feel it pulsating, *ba-dum, ba-dum, ba-dum*? If you can answer "yes" to either of the questions above, then you have some measure of a glory deficiency. It is our ubiquitous human reality.

Even if you have had a deep-seated revelation of who God is, how much He loves you, and how He sees you, you probably still need to grow in this area. Our quest for glory runs deep.

The problems resulting from a glory deficiency can be recognized and largely understood without bringing "religion" into the picture. When I read of treatment programs that seek to cure the ills of society, I see vestiges of the gospel but without God Himself. Unconditional love. Treating people with dignity. Imparting a sense of worth. Developing personal connections. All are Biblically based parts of the humanistic process. I will not malign these efforts if they prevent violence and help free people from addictions, but even the best approaches are merely nibbling around the edges of true meaning, transformation, and purpose. They have potential to bring a degree of change but lack the eternal benefits of knowing God.

I think most humanists recognize the destructive power of shame. That is why they promote playing games without keeping score, giving out participation trophies, enforcing speech codes, and smothering young people with messages to believe in themselves. There was even an elementary school that, to teach kindness and encourage inclusion, would not allow sixth-grade girls to say "no" if asked by a boy to dance at the annual Valentine's Day party. What a precedent for life that approach sets! With public pressure mounting, the administration decided that a policy change was warranted.[1]

The premise behind such an approach is that if we can successfully prevent the causes of shame, people will be emotionally healthy. Such efforts, however, tend to create even more societal dysfunction because removing "shame triggers" often leaves a wake of socially destructive attitudes of entitlement. Regardless of how people are treated, the "I will ascend" motivation of the human heart will always produce its insidious fruit. Whether by ignorance or choice, secular wisdom seems to miss this piece of the human puzzle.

Ours is a cruel world, and we can never entirely avoid criticism or prevent efforts to shame. Instead, we need strength to withstand our trials. Such fortitude comes not just from within ourselves, but from being unconditionally loved by others. A healthy family can add a measure of strength and stability, but only the unconditional love of God will truly satisfy our deep-rooted glory deficiencies and make us firmly secure in who we are. Ultimately, the only healthy way to find real significance—and all the benefits that go with it—is through a covenant relationship with the King of Glory.

Emulating Jesus is certainly a good idea; His life stands as the greatest example throughout all of human history. Even so, we are not brought into wholeness by the principles of Jesus, but rather by our connection to His *presence* (i.e., glory). If you know that presence,

---

1. Christina Zdanowicz, "A school catches flak for telling girls they can't say no if a boy asks them to dance," CNN, updated February 13, 2018, accessed April 02, 2024, https://www.cnn.com/2018/02/13/health/utah-school-children-dance-trnd/index.html.

I encourage you to draw nearer to Him and deeper into His truth, because as you have probably already realized, there is more to this Christian life than we are generally led to believe.

The fact that God's glory is *invisible* to the natural eye can complicate our struggles. This difficulty, I know well. While in my thirties, I left the apparent security of a career in chemistry to pursue college ministry as a vocation. Having two elementary-aged children did not make the decision easier. I then left that fruitful work to pioneer a new ministry. From a natural perspective, these choices have been foolish ones. Trust me; living by faith as a means of financial provision has not felt glorious. But even though my choices might appear foolish, by His grace the Lord has lavished my family with spiritual wealth beyond human comprehension. In all likelihood, though, it will not be until the "day of appraisal" mentioned earlier that my life choices make sense to others.

With glory, a similar principle applies. Because God's glory is spiritual, it is also *unseen*. Thus, those who embrace eternal grandeur will appear as Ichabods in the eyes of the world. *As Christians, we have been glorified, we are being glorified, and we will be glorified, but the revealing of this magnificent splendor is for a future time.*

Jesus gave us a glimpse of His glorious reality on the mount of transfiguration (Matthew 17:1–8), but not even Christ's intimate friends recognized His true splendor until it was privately revealed on the mountain. In a similar sense, the glory of Christ's followers will remain hidden until the kingdom of God comes in its fullness.

The quest for true glory, I think you can see, requires *courage*. Not the courage needed to step onto a battlefield, but courage to face the battle going on within our own souls; courage to confront our shortcomings and weaknesses, courage to humble our pride, and courage to go against the flow of human opinion. Such bravery is more than worthy of our pursuit.

Spiritual glory is by no means powerless simply because it is invisible to the natural eye. True, substantive glory forms the foundation for real freedom. Those who embrace our Creator's grace-based plan for glorification find freedom from the need to measure up to law-based standards for both kingdom and social righteousness. This Spirit-breathed liberty also translates into freedom from pride, freedom from shame, freedom from guilt, and freedom from condemnation.

Perhaps the greatest freedom of all involves being released from the innate "I will ascend" compulsion that has plagued humanity since Adam and Eve gave ear to the deceptive hiss of the serpent. In so many ways, the Christian gospel not only reverses the tragedy of Eden, it also prevents anything like it from ever happening again. The Son of Man has wisely set the stage for a magnificent unveiling in heaven. Because of what Jesus has done, the ultimate temptation will end in ichabod failure.

Just as I began this book by highlighting the contrast between the pseudo-substance of human glory and the weighty significance of divine glory, so too must I emphasize the contrast between the world's promises and God's. The voices of this world forever promise fulfillment, wholeness, and significance, but they speak shallow lies. Try to grasp the world's promises in your hand, and they will slip through your fingers like dry sand.

We can spend our entire lives chasing shadows of glory, but there is no true significance apart from a covenant relationship with the ever-sovereign King of Glory. We are because He is. And because He is who He is, we are people of value, worth, and significance. We have been glorified, are being glorified, and will be glorified—of this you can be certain. On the playground of life, we might be outcasts, but on a day sure to come, everyone will want to be us.

QUESTIONS

1. Why is it dangerous to attempt to replicate the effects of the gospel without Jesus?

2. Why is merely removing "shame triggers" problematic?

3. How does obtaining true glory set us free?

FURTHER READING: Matthew 17:1–8 and Romans 8:18–25

PRAYER: Lord, please open my eyes to see Your glory, and grant me the courage to go against the tide of human pride.

DAY FORTY
HEARTS OF WORSHIP

Men of low degree are only vanity and men of rank are a lie;
In the balances they go up;
They are together lighter than breath.

Psalm 62:9

We have accounts of the deification of men in pagan mythology. But I do not remember any account of a god becoming a man, to help man. Whoever heard of Jupiter or Mars or Minerva coming down and attempting to bear the burdens of men? The gods were willing enough to receive the gifts of men, but Christianity is unique in the fact that our God became a man with human infirmity and emptied Himself of the glory of heaven, in order that He might take upon Himself the sins, diseases and weakness of our humanity.

—A. C. Dixon

On March 15, 44 BC, Julius Caesar—the ruler of the Roman Republic—was assassinated by a group of senators. In the chaos that followed, Caesar's adopted heir, Octavian, consolidated power by defeating opposing leaders in battle and killing a potential competitor for the throne. Octavian then had Julius Caesar deified and proclaimed himself to be "the son of the deified" (or "the son of the divine"). Taking the name Augustus Caesar, he also declared himself to be emperor. Thus began the mighty Roman Empire.

It was during this season of Roman prosperity that Jesus—the supposedly illegitimate son of Joseph and Mary—was born in a stable. Unlike Emperor Augustus and local King Herod, Jesus quietly bided His time with little public recognition. When the Messiah did step out of obscurity into the public eye, His "entourage" consisted mainly of ordinary men with no wealth or social standing.

The Bible tells us that Jesus was indeed the King of kings and Lord of lords, the very Son of God. Even so, taking ownership of the *Son of Man* title, He lowered Himself time after time for the sake of others—even the untouchables. This humility was not simply an image displayed to garner popular favor, but rather a true representation of His humble and loving nature.

Humankind decorates its political and religious landscapes with public portrayals of pious devotion and generosity, but pitifully few travel the road of true humility. People ever attempt to usurp the glory of God, and exceptions are nonexistent.

Like a solar eclipse, humanity moves to blot out the Son. We can never forget, though, that the moon's light is but a reflection of the sun's. Human significance might appear to be as large and brilliant as God's glory for a short while, but it is only an illusion. Attempting to obscure our Creator will only bring darkness to ourselves. God's glory fills the cosmos and will eventually cover the earth regardless of how high we attempt to lift ourselves. This truth was demonstrated when Jesus' ragtag band of followers grew in strength, and without sword or bow, overthrew the mighty Roman Empire.

From the moment of His first breath until His final cry on the cross, the Son of Man triumphed over the ultimate temptation. Never once did the prideful cry of "I will ascend!" echo in His heart. For our benefit, Jesus gave up the glory that He rightly deserved. In doing so, Christ demonstrated that He is indeed worthy of *all* glory.

> Have this attitude in yourselves which was also in Christ Jesus, who, although He existed in the form of God, did not regard equality with God a thing to be grasped, but emptied Himself, taking the form of a bond-servant, and being made in the likeness of men. Being found in appearance as a man, He humbled Himself by becoming obedient to the point of death, even death on a cross. For this reason also, God highly exalted Him, and bestowed on Him the name which is above every name, so that at the name of Jesus every knee will bow, of those who are in heaven and on earth and under the earth, and that every tongue will confess that Jesus Christ is Lord, to the glory of God the Father. Philippians 2:5–11

Why do we worship God?[1] *Because He alone is worthy.* Only He can be the center of the universe without becoming self-centered. Only He can reign without controlling. And only He can receive glory without becoming enamored with Himself. On the contrary, time after time, humanity has displayed its inability to handle glory. Whether we speak of a political leader proclaiming his supremacy, an athlete vaunting her success, or an academic enthralled with his intellectual savvy, the pursuit of glory is both ubiquitous and toxic. We want it desperately, but we cannot handle it.

God has a solution to our plight! Yes, He begins by revealing our glory deficiency, but then He gives both a new heart and a new identity. Finally, He gives us reason to channel glory back to Him. This process helps us to "renew our minds," to break old patterns of thought and establish new ones (Romans 12:1–2). Failure to follow this divine pattern can lead to what I call "the pride-affliction cycle."

We naturally seek to exalt ourselves, but pride comes before the fall. When life is good and we feel we are doing well, our egos begin to swell. Thus, we set ourselves up to be humbled by our circumstances. Before long, we will wrestle with afflictions and feelings of inadequacy. God is opposed to the proud, but He also gives grace to the afflicted (James 4:6). So, He lovingly reaches down and lifts us out of our pit of misery. Feeling better about ourselves and our circumstances, we then proceed to repeat the cycle all over again. For some of us, the pride-affliction cycle is a way of life.

When we are doing well, thoughts of elation and significance bubble to the surface of both heart and mind. These responses are natural but become problematic when we try to own the glory for ourselves. The secret to breaking the cycle lies in learning to turn the glory back to God.

None of us are worthy of glory in and of ourselves. All that we have and all that we are flows from His throne of mercy and grace. It is only reasonable, then, that we channel thankfulness, worship, and praise back to the rightful source of all splendor: our Creator.

As we align ourselves with heaven's divine reality, God begins to mysteriously "clothe" us with His glory. As already stated, we

---

1. Understanding the dynamics of the Trinity (Godhead) can be difficult, but the basic idea is that there is no difference in character or nature between the Father, Son, and Holy Spirit. Thus, what the Son accomplished reflects the entire Trinity.

can receive glory, but we cannot take it. We can receive glory as an unearned gift from our Creator, but we cannot reach out and take it for ourselves. Thus, our boast must be in God and not in ourselves.

The King of Glory does not need our worship. He is self-existent, all-powerful, and replete with magnificent splendor. *We, however, need to worship Him.* Not only because He is worthy, but because it is the only way that we can overcome the ultimate temptation.

When we think of being tested, thoughts of adversity usually come to mind, but the Bible says that we are also tested by the praise given us (Proverbs 27:21). If you truly want to experience God's fullness, you had better prepare yourself to receive praise as well as criticism. There is no need to be weird or artificially humble. If someone compliments you, graciously thank the person, but then use that opportunity to minister to the Lord by thanking Him for His goodness in your life.

Spiritually perceptive hearts recognize the contrast between their unworthiness and our Creator's fathomless splendor. Knowing full well that we were dead-dog sinners whom Christ has lifted up to sit in heavenly places, worship is, above all, an act of love and appreciation.

The Son of God became the Son of Man so the sons of men could become glorious sons of God. For this, we are ever thankful! It is a testimony of God's greatness that some people would rather die for the sake of His glory than preserve their lives for their own.

QUESTIONS

1. What did Jesus accomplish that no other human could?

2. Why is it vital for Christians to renew their minds and develop new thought patterns?

3. What should we do when thoughts of glory begin to fill our minds?

FURTHER READING: Luke 2:1–14 and Philippians 3

PRAYER: Lord, You alone are worthy of glory and honor. May praise and worship be the natural inclinations of my heart!

PHASE FOUR REFLECTIONS

In a mystery beyond comprehension, the Creator of the Universe chooses to reside within human vessels. He is also building us together into an amazing temple of "living stones" so that, together as a loving community of believers, we might display His glory. The Lord is indeed our hope of glory. (Day 31)

God's people also form a royal priesthood that focuses on ministering to the Lord first and to people second. Others do not always appreciate our efforts to help them, but when our first ministry is to the Lord, we can endure neglect, criticism, and even persecution because we know that He sees and values the true intentions of our hearts. The King of Glory will never forget the service that we do in His honor. (Day 32)

The Bible identifies the church as the bride of Christ. By design, the marriage covenant paints for us an image of this relationship. Jesus is not motivated by a sterile, dutiful sense of responsibility, but rather by an intense, passionate love for His bride. All of heaven is counting down the days until we are forever joined with our Lord and Savior. (Day 33)

Becoming a Christian means that we are transferred from the kingdom of darkness into the kingdom of God's beloved Son. And not only do we become citizens of the kingdom of God, we also become ambassadors for Christ who serve as ministers of reconciliation. What an honor God has given us to influence others for eternity! (Day 34)

The value of an earthly inheritance will last for only a short while. All who become children of God, however, become joint heirs with Jesus, and these blessed individuals are destined to receive an eternal inheritance beyond our imagination. The down payment of this inheritance—the Holy Spirit dwelling in our hearts—is amazing within itself. (Day 35)

In an irony beyond all ironies, God not only saves us from our sins, He also lifts us up to be seated with Christ in heavenly places. Earthly kings show a history of doing the opposite, often killing those they view as potential threats to their thrones. We all proved ourselves to be dead-dog sinners by joining Lucifer's nefarious coup against God and His kingdom, but Jesus saved us anyway. God has given an amazing gift of honor to those who deserved only wrath. (Day 36)

The dynamics of being saved and elevated by God run contrary to our natural ways of thinking. One of humanity's biggest mistakes involves our incorrect perception of weakness. Collectively, we despise weakness because it increases the potential for public humiliation. From a kingdom perspective, however, weakness helps to prepare our hearts to humbly receive the amazing power of God's transformational grace. Times of weakness, struggle, and adversity are not signs that God has abandoned us. Rather, they provide opportunities for us to put off old mindsets and put on new. (Day 37)

Despising weakness, we naturally tend to seek success in an effort to cover past abuses, failures, and inadequacies. However, college degrees, vocational success, and high social status are powerless to heal our brokenness. The real secret to wholeness lies not in lifting ourselves up, but in connecting with God by lowering ourselves to journey along the "high road" of humility. (Day 38)

Secular society's solution to overcoming the toxic effects of shame is to eliminate "shame triggers" entirely. But not only is it impossible to remove all sources of shame, humanistic attempts to create positive self-images also create attitudes of entitlement. Our heavenly Father promises to remove our shame, but not by inflating our egos. Only through His unconditional love and the wisdom of the gospel can we be freed from the toxic effects of shame while also remaining humble in our hearts. (Day 39)

Devoted Christians are often prone to being caught in a frustrating trap that we can identify as the "pride-affliction cycle." When doing well, we tend to pridefully lift our heads in self-glorification. With pride inevitably leading to a fall, we then find ourselves wallowing in negative emotions and crying out to God for help. The Lord has provided a better way for us. One of the secrets to handling the euphoria of success involves simply turning the glory back to God through praise, worship, and thanksgiving. We know that we would have nothing if it were not for Him, and that in Him, we have all that we need. (Day 40)

FINAL REFLECTIONS

Experiencing the disparity of economic extremes can wreak havoc on a person's perspective. For example, someone who takes a mission trip from a prosperous culture to one marked by extreme poverty is likely to face all kinds of reverse culture shock upon their return. So many things that were once idolized can suddenly seem frivolous.

Such an individual might feel guilty eating at a pricey restaurant, find sporting events to be hollow, and sink into frustration because others seem oblivious to the disparity. "Don't these people know that children are starving to death while they eat expensive meals, spend a fortune on entertainment, and complain about everything?"

After the initial shock of returning, a "new normal" begins to emerge. A few people might cope by blocking out the memory of human suffering and moving on with their lives as though the trip never happened. Many more, however, will adjust their lifestyles. While still enjoying some of life's pleasures, they will change their spending habits and steer newly conserved resources to those in need. They might even take additional steps to broadcast the need and rally others to the cause. In other words, their eye-opening experience will create a vision to make a difference in this world, and they will align their lives to bring that vision to fulfillment.

A similar process might take place when your eyes are opened to the disparity between human and divine glory. At least, that has been my personal experience. I wrote and edited this book during a time "rich" in sporting events for those living in the United States. As I saw stadiums filled with cheering fans and grand ceremonies celebrating human glory, I felt conflicted. I wanted to enjoy the excitement, but so much of it seemed empty and shallow. What was I to do? After all, the Olympic luge competition is awesome—not to mention curling and short track racing!

When God opens your eyes to the reality of His kingdom, an internal conflict will likely result. This inner angst indicates that it might be time for you to develop a new normal, to learn how to be spiritually fruitful while living in a wayward world. *Becoming hypercritical does not help.* By developing a new normal, you can still participate in—and enjoy—many seemingly frivolous activities for the purposes of recreation, building relationships, and influencing others for the glory of God. Three basic, related steps will help you move forward in your growth. Each step builds upon the other with the final result being a life well lived.

First, take time to process the concepts related to glory and identity. These issues go to the roots of who you are, so they need repeated, long-term attention. Becoming aware is only the beginning. You also need to pray, read, contemplate, and pray some more. I recommend working through this book again or finding other Biblically based resources that address similar issues. Of course, use these resources in conjunction with the Scriptures. As you take time to meditate on God's truth, your mind will be renewed, and your thought processes will begin to change.

Second, along with renewing your mind, you must align your actions with God's design. As you seek God's face and grow in His grace, He will prompt you to take steps that follow His calling for your life. It might mean breaking off some old relationships and forging new ones. Or it may require reevaluating the amount of time, money, and energy you spend on goods and activities with little or no lasting value. Or maybe you will need to discipline your thoughts, putting off feelings of pride or insecurity while purposefully turning glory back to the only One who is worthy.

Finally, as you learn and grow, the Lord will give you a "sphere of influence." This sphere is specific to you because no one else has the same unique mix of experiences, abilities, and relationships. It does not matter whether your past has been successful or regretful, you are an ambassador for Christ, and there are people you can influence with love, truth, and hope. Regardless of whether your platform is a school, a business office, or even a jail cell, do not despise your circumstances. Use them for the benefit of others!

Trust me; if you are walking with God, learning His ways, and growing into His likeness, you have something to offer. Ultimately, life is not about you, but about allowing the Lord to work through you. As a Spirit-empowered child of God, a royal priest, and an ambassador for Christ, you can do whatever He calls you to do!

APPENDIX

Becoming a Christian means entering into a sacred and binding covenant relationship with the King of Glory and becoming a subject of His kingdom. This is not a step to be taken lightly, but the gospel does present an amazing, hope-filled opportunity for those willing to admit that they have been living contrary to God's design.

People often question God's goodness because He has made salvation exclusive to the new covenant of Jesus, rather than allowing everyone to simply traipse into heaven. But for those who have not been cleansed of their sins, eternally experiencing the weight and intensity of God's holy glory would present an unbearable state of agony beyond comprehension. Thankfully, the Father's arms are extended wide for all who genuinely desire to become members of His royal family.

If you have never entered into a sacred covenant with God through faith in Christ, I encourage you to earnestly seek Him. Pray for the King of Glory to reveal Himself to you. Search the Scriptures for truth that touches your soul. If you have doubts, ask questions and search out answers. If people chide you for asking, continue to ask regardless. Knowing God is far more important than pleasing people, and knowing requires asking questions. Otherwise, you will never be able to explore the depths of the Almighty.

Because we have all sinned against the benevolent King of the Universe, we are all spiritual debtors. Ask Jesus to forgive you and invite Him to be your Lord and Savior. There is nothing you need to do to make yourself worthy. Faith in Christ's sacrificial death and resurrection is all you need.

As you seek God, also learn to cultivate deeper faith. Every aspect of the Christian life requires faith. We begin with belief in Christ's deity and resurrection, and learn to trust Him in every area of our lives. When faith is lacking, true, substantive glory will never be realized to its fullest.

Trusting your Savior enables you to surrender to His will. Two powerful purposes are then accomplished. First, you humble yourself when you let go of control. Second, you invite the wise Creator of all things to have sway in your life. That is never a bad idea.

The Christian life involves an individual walk with God, but His glory is fully realized only as we connect with a healthy community of believers. If you have not already done so, find a good local church—one with a solid understanding of grace—and be sure to get water baptized as a public declaration of your faith.

Throughout the centuries, well-meaning people have mistaken the Bible as a book full of rules. Yes, the old covenant given by Moses was law-based, but under the new covenant in Christ, the law of love is now the driving force that governs our lives.[1] If you learn and live the wisdom of God's love, you will do well, and He will be pleased.

The Christian life is unnatural; it moves against the tide of our individual tendencies and violates many of our collective norms. Furthermore, while the dark forces of hell try to pull you back into their inglorious pit, our gracious God will work to purge your self-centered dysfunction. This combination of elements means that you will sometimes feel as though you are pushed to the limit of what you can bear. Fear not! Your heavenly Father intends the process to refine and not destroy you. You will one day see and know the fullness of His glory if you allow Him to write the end of your story.

The Bible will always be integral to the process of coming to know and walk with God. No other book on earth compares to this Spirit-inspired expression of our Creator's incredible intelligence. If you are new to the Scriptures, you might want to check out *The TouchPoint: Connecting with God through the Bible*. I wrote the book primarily as an introduction to the Scriptures for those seeking to develop a deeper relationship with their Creator.

Much more can and has been said about the Christian experience, but knowledge is merely a stepping stone to greater things. Ultimately, growing in faith and love for God, seeking His wisdom, and connecting with His people form the core of the dynamic Christian experience.[2] Hold on to your hat because the adventure is just beginning, and the best is yet to come!

---

1. My book *The Divine Progression of Grace: Blazing a Trail to Fruitful Living* provides an in-depth explanation of the relationship between law and grace.
2. *Say Goodbye to Regret: Discovering the Secret to a Blessed Life* provides a basic understanding of God's wisdom and how to obtain it.

ACKNOWLEDGMENTS

I so appreciate all who lovingly invested their precious time and effort into this project! My name is on the front cover of this book, but I could not do what I do without the help of caring and generous people.

Johanna Beatty, Jason Betler, Tom Brazell, Joe Canton, Jr., Deb Croyle, Jeff Ference, Jason Hutchins, Ricky Ingram, Joe Jansen, Lynda Logue, Samantha Mitchell, Dustin Musser, Steve Rhoades, Elaine Rice, Rose Salazar, Debi Santos, and Jen Tillson all played vital roles in helping me through the more tedious aspects of formulating ideas, writing, and editing. Crystal Min of crystalclearenglish.com provided input as an editor that was over the top and invaluable.

Debi Adams, Samantha Carey, Carl Forster, Matt Geppert, Gary Ham, Sandy Hempfling, Josh Rendulic, and JP Sprecher graciously carved time out of their busy schedules to write endorsements.

Chris and Cynthia Leidlein took a fun adventure with Debi and me for a photo shoot while at a conference in Florida. (What patient spouses Cynthia and I have!) K-Lee Gaffney then did a terrific job turning our photos into a meaningful cover. Stacy Bates, Steve Margita, and Bernie Wilke also contributed their expertise as I worked out my design ideas.

Finally, a special thanks goes to those who support the life-changing work of Search for Me Ministries, Inc. The resources we publish are tangible expressions of their unseen love and faithfulness.

ABOUT THE AUTHOR

Bob Santos writes to see lives transformed by God's goodness. Years of working in college ministry revealed that people crave to know more about God not only in their hearts through faith, but also through a deeper understanding of the truths found in His Word.

Pursuing spiritual vitality, Bob helps others "connect the dots" of Biblical truth by addressing "missing links" of contemporary theology. In this, Bob's books and video teachings explore key Biblical themes—such as covenants, grace, identity, rest, unity, and wisdom—that are often misunderstood or widely ignored. His explanations of difficult concepts, combined with inspirational messages of hope in Christ, are insightful, thought-provoking, and transformational as they explore the Christian faith in an understandable and yet intellectually satisfying way.

Bob was licensed for Christian ministry in 1997 and ordained in 2005 through Elim Fellowship (www.elimfellowship.org). In 2006, Bob and his wife Debi founded Search for Me Ministries, Inc. (sfme.org) with the mission to help form and equip a generation of world changers for Christ through the production of Biblically-based teaching resources.

College sweethearts, Bob and Debi have been married for over forty years. They have two adult children, two grandchildren, and three granddogs. When he is not writing, speaking, or leading a Bible study, you will likely find Bob doing something in the great outdoors.

ADDITIONAL RESOURCES FROM SEARCH FOR ME MINISTRIES

Additional copies of *From Glory to Glory* can be purchased through major online retailers. Volume discounts are also available for ministry organizations through SfMe Media (www.sfme.org). (Audiobook available)

Deciding what to teach and preach about can present a significant challenge for pastors and ministry leaders. *The Teleios Trail: Thirty Topics to Explore for Spiritual Growth* is an excellent resource to help grow spiritually mature disciples of Christ.

Division has long plagued the church, reflecting badly on Christianity and hindering our mission. *Greater Glory: The Transformational Power of Christian Unity* challenges us to embrace God's perspective so we can live out the lifestyle of love that is central to our faith. (Audiobook available)

There is a profound logic behind all that God does, but it is not human logic. *The Age of Abiding: Experiencing the Life of the Vine* provides powerful insights into human nature, helping the reader better grasp the mysterious beauty of the Christian gospel. (Audiobook available)

The Search for Rest: Fifty Days to a More Peaceful Life provides an awesome personal or group study that explores the concept of the Sabbath from both spiritual and physical perspectives. This thought-provoking book meets a powerful need in a world that is filled with anxiety and unrest. (Audiobook available)

Much of the Christian faith makes little sense to the modern, Western mind because the Bible was written with a mentality that differs from current thought. *Drinking Truth: Embracing the Covenant Mindset of the Bible* provides an insightful look at the new covenant in light of the covenantal mindset with which the Bible was penned. (Audiobook available)

The ***Community Prayer Devotional*** is a powerful book that brings churches together to pray. Even better, the cover can be personalized to fit your community, allowing people to take ownership and embrace prayer as a lifestyle! (Audiobook available)

Say Goodbye to Regret: Discovering the Secret to a Blessed Life is a life-changing book that deals with the problem of regret on two fronts. Learn how to move beyond the lingering pain of regret and also how to avoid regrets entirely by pursuing the rich treasures of God's spiritual wisdom. (Audiobook available)

The TouchPoint: Connecting with God through the Bible is a valuable resource for those who are interested in learning more about the Bible. Revised in 2020, this book provides a great introduction to the Christian Scriptures while emphasizing a personal relationship with God. (Audiobook available)

The Divine Progression of Grace: Blazing a Trail to Fruitful Living thoughtfully explores God's grace from a perspective of empowerment as well as acceptance. This book will take you deeper into a relationship with your Creator and also help make you more usable for His purposes.

Each reading in ***Champions in the Wilderness: Fifty-Two Devotions to Guide and Strengthen Emerging Overcomers*** draws from a deep well of truth to encourage, strengthen, and instruct those who desire to walk with God but are struggling in the face of adversity. The format of this devotional lends itself well to group discussion. (Audiobook available)

POSTING BOOK REVIEWS

Please consider posting an online review of this book. Honest reviews are deeply appreciated and provide an easy way for our readers to contribute to our ministry efforts. Also, if your life has been touched by one of our resources, please recommend it to others.

SFME MEDIA

SfMe Media belongs to Search for Me Ministries, Inc. (SfMe Ministries)—an IRS-recognized 501(c)(3) nonprofit organization. Search for Me Ministries burns with a vision to help form and equip a generation of world changers for Christ. We believe in the importance of reaching those who do not know the Lord, but we also recognize the need for healthy churches as landing places for new believers. By helping Christians grow to maturity with our uniquely flavored teaching resources, we are helping to create environments that foster the fulfilment of the Great Commission in every way.

www.ingramcontent.com/pod-product-compliance
Lightning Source LLC
Chambersburg PA
CBHW071732080526
44588CB00013B/1998